Strengthening Library Ecosystems

STRENGTHENING LIBRARY ECOSYSTEMS

Collaborate for Advocacy and Impact

DORCAS HAND, SARA KELLY JOHNS,
MICHELLE ROBERTSON, & ERYN DUFFEE

ALA Editions
CHICAGO | 2024

Extensive effort has gone into ensuring the reliability of the information in this book; however, the publisher makes no warranty, express or implied, with respect to the material contained herein.

ISBN: 979-8-89255-572-2 (paper)

Library of Congress Cataloging-in-Publication Data

Names: Hand, Dorcas, author. | Johns, Sara Kelly, author. | Robertson, Michelle, Ph. D., author. | Duffee, Eryn, author.
Title: Strengthening library ecosystems : collaborate for advocacy and impact / Dorcas Hand, Sara Kelly Johns, Michelle Robertson, and Eryn Duffee.
Description: Chicago : ALA Editions, 2024. | Includes bibliographical references and index.
Identifiers: LCCN 2024013907 | ISBN 9798892555722 (paperback)
Subjects: LCSH: Library cooperation—United States. | Libraries and community—United States. | Libraries—Aims and objectives—United States. | Libraries—Public relations—United States. | Libraries—Political aspects—United States. | Libraries—Societies, etc.
Classification: LCC Z672.13.U6 H36 2024 | DDC 021.6/4—dc23/eng20240510
LC record available at https://lccn.loc.gov/2024013907

Cover design by Kim Hudgins. Composition design by Alejandra Diaz in the Lust Text and Effra typefaces.

♾ This paper meets the requirements of ANSI/NISO Z39.48-1992 (Permanence of Paper).

Printed in the United States of America
28 27 26 25 24   5 4 3 2 1

CONTENTS

Preface, by Dorcas Hand **vii**

Introduction **xi**

PART I | **The Ecosystem Foundation**

1 What Is a Library Ecosystem?..*3*
Sara Kelly Johns

2 Uniting Around Core Values and Common Goals.....................*15*
Dorcas Hand

PART II | **Elements of Ecosystem Thinking**

3 Understanding the Four Pillars of the Continuum.....................*29*
Dorcas Hand

4 Ecosystem Leadership: Beginning, Building, and Sustaining ...*49*
Michelle Robertson

5 Progress Requires Strong Communication *55*
Eryn Duffee

6 Collaboration Builds Success *65*
Sara Kelly Johns

7 Sustaining Your Advocacy Ecosystem *77*
Dorcas Hand

PART III | **Applying Ecosystem Ideas**

8 Advocacy: Leading from Life...*87*
Anthony Chow

9 Leveraging the Ecosystem for Effective
Legislative Advocacy *99*
Eryn Duffee

10   Ecosystem Warriors Stand Together
for Intellectual Freedom *111*
Barbara K. Stripling

PART IV | **Many Kinds of Library Advocates**

11   Academic Libraries Need the Library Ecosystem................... *135*
Rachel Minkin and Jennifer Dean

12   School Libraries Are Pillars in Library Ecosystems *145*
Kathy Lester

13   Public Libraries Reach Everyone............................... *163*
Jen Alvino Wood

14   Potential Partners in Library Ecosystems *173*
Sara Kelly Johns

15   Diverse Advocates Championing Libraries *181*
Dorcas Hand

16   Library Ecosystem Leadership at the State Level *191*
Dorcas Hand

PART V | **Ecosystems in Action**

17   Five Ecosystem Journeys... *201*
Michelle Robertson

18   The Myth of Going It Alone *211*
Megan Cusick

Conclusion: One Voice, One Future, by Eryn Duffee and
Michelle Robertson **221**

APPENDIXES
Appendix A: The Ecosystem Agenda Building Templates **225**
Appendix B: State and Local Year-Round Advocacy Checklist **235**
Appendix C: A Comparison of Public, School, and Academic Libraries:
Vital to Our Communities **237**
Appendix D: Additional Resources **241**

About the Authors and Contributors **247**
Index **251**

PREFACE

Dorcas Hand

For as long as I have been a librarian, I worked in the world of school libraries—but I relied on my ALA membership to keep me aware of trends in other library types that might impact my work, or from which I could learn new methods. ALA and the world of librarianship are huge worlds, and it was clear to me that I was happiest in my own silo of school libraries. And then I began to serve on ALA committees, to expand my involvement in the wider world of libraries rather than just observing it. Working with librarians from other types of libraries deepened my understanding of our commonalities and facilitated my work leading the original Ecosystem Initiative Task Force. Together we wrote the ALA Ecosystem Toolkit that is available now (see www.ala.org/advocacy/ala-ecosystem-initiative). Since 2020, the ALA Committee on Library Advocacy's (COLA's) Ecosystem Subcommittee has worked to promote the toolkit to groups within and beyond ALA in order to support stronger advocacy by libraries by encouraging greater collaboration among them. When we stand together at any level—local, state, or national—our voice is stronger.

How the Ecosystem Initiative Began

ALA's Ecosystem Initiative aims to encourage all types of libraries to collaborate on advocacy efforts The idea for the initiative came out of efforts by the American Association of School Librarians (AASL) to support the inclusion of school libraries in the funding stream of Obama's 2015 Every Student Succeeds Act (ESSA). Because this was the first federal act that named school libraries as eligible for funds, and because every state handles the planning process of applying for federal grants differently, AASL set up a series of workshops in over forty states to help school librarians develop the relationships they needed to convince their state leadership, and particularly the state departments of education, to include school libraries in their plans when applying for grants. Those workshops pushed the idea that libraries are an *ecosystem*, that all library types can work together to support each other, and that all libraries would benefit if school libraries were stronger. Those stronger school libraries would feed new patrons to public libraries even during those students' K-12 careers, to college and university libraries as they graduated, and to law, medical and other special libraries as those K-12 students graduated to more adult pursuits.

The Ecosystem Initiative has been developed under the aegis of ALA, which means ALA hopes it will be useful to ALA members and affiliates in supporting strong advocacy at all levels. That said, *anyone* can use these tools and ideas to further their own library advocacy efforts. ALA is not overseeing any specific ecosystem efforts or expecting any particular results. It also means that your ecosystem team members will want to take advantage of any other available ALA resources as you move your own projects forward. The Ecosystem Toolkit is intended for independent use by all interested library stakeholders.

Jim Rettig first used the term "ecosystem" in the context of libraries in 2008 or so, and Jim Neal brought the term up again about the same time as this ESSA effort came about. The job of our Ecosystem Initiative Task Force was to use these ideas to develop a toolkit to be rolled out across ALA during its annual meeting in 2019.

Once the Ecosystem Toolkit had been posted to the ALA website, the focus turned to its implementation. Starting in 2020, ALA's ecosystem team has presented the toolkit at various state conferences and affiliate groups. That variety of audiences has helped us clarify how to discuss ecosystem ideas in better ways, and to develop stronger tools for users to apply. This book reflects much of that work. Why do ecosystem ideas matter to you? And why do these ideas matter to our patrons and communities?

FIGURE 0.1 | **Library types' advocates and supporters**

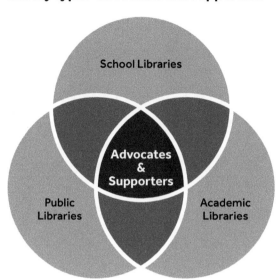

We were such a team, the initial writers of the Ecosystem Toolkit. We wrestled first with what being an ecosystem means, and then with how to offer specific methods to support building an advocacy network that included all library types. We came from many different states and all different library types ourselves, so we had the basics in our group—but sorting through the many possibilities to find benchmarks and language that would resonate with our national library community was challenging—and exciting.

And now we offer this work to you, in a comprehensive book to support your future efforts to speak across library types with *One Voice* that moves everyone forward.

INTRODUCTION

Ecosystem. The very idea is inclusive and cooperative. In biodynamic terms, the ecosystem that supports our Mother Earth has been successful for eons. This book offers readers tools and ideas that support increased cooperation and collaboration across libraries, including all types as well as their supporters, in hopes that you will establish ecosystem initiatives that can endure current and future crises. We, the editorial team, think it is time to help you readers—librarians and library supporters—reach beyond your silos and library comfort zones to energize the library ecosystem that already exists, and thus inspire stronger and more successful advocacy initiatives. Please join our great adventure. This book consists of the following parts:

Part I, "The Ecosystem Foundation," explains what a library ecosystem is and how it can work. We also offer you an understanding of what all libraries have in common, knowledge sometimes lost in our busy everyday lives.

Part II, "Elements of Ecosystem Thinking," dives into the Ecosystem Continuum rubric and its four pillars: leadership, communication, collaboration, and sustainability.

Part III, "Applying Ecosystem Ideas," illustrates how ecosystem thinking can strengthen advocacy generally. Legislative advocacy illustrates one application of ecosystem ideas. And finally, we consider how ecosystem thinking can contribute to more robust responses to censorship efforts.

Part IV, "Many Kinds of Library Advocates," offers an understanding of how the various library types (school, public, and academic) differ, and how they can better see one another as essential allies in our work. We also consider some related groups, like trustees, Friends, foundations, state libraries, and more. All of these groups support strong libraries in their states and regions and would like to be included in ecosystem efforts.

Part V, "Ecosystems in Action," offers the flip sides of a final coin. First, we examine a few case studies of ecosystem initiatives that already exist to illustrate how different they are, and how they made some of the choices they did in proceeding toward their specific advocacy agendas. And then we hear what happens when there is no ecosystem, no cross-collaboration, but only independent actions that are less effective.

The book concludes with a set of appendixes. The "Ecosystem Agenda Building Templates" (appendix A) will guide groups in the process of developing a collaborative agenda. Appendix B includes the "Local Year-Round Advocacy Checklist," another useful template to help teams plan ahead to have what they need at the times their deadlines are approaching. These documents are elements of the overarching Toolkit.

We refer often to the "Comparison of Public, School, and Academic Libraries: Vital to Our Communities" (appendix C). This document will help everyone see how much the three main library types have in common, as well as how their missions differ in important ways.

The final appendix, appendix D, contains additional resources that can help to strengthen collaborative efforts among local library advocates.

For a general description of ALA's Ecosystem Initiative, see the website "ALA Ecosystem Initiative: ONE VOICE: Building a Strong Library Ecosystem" (www.ala.org/advocacy/ala-ecosystem-initiative), which offers links to webinars and presentations from various states. Poke around for lots of ideas to support your deepest understanding of how to build an ecosystem that does what your team needs done.

We find the nuances of ecosystem work to be both fascinating and incredibly useful on the ground in daily efforts to improve the public's understanding of what libraries do, as well as in legislative advocacy as libraries come together to enlist support at the state, federal, or even local levels. We hope you will find these ideas enticing and concretely useful, and that you will be motivated to reach out to colleagues across your own ecosystem, whether you knew you had one before today or not. You can start a brand-new group with these new understandings, or you can take these ideas to your existing advocacy team or state library organization and reinvigorate their current methods.

May the Ecosystem Force be with you!

PART I

The Ecosystem Foundation

1

WHAT IS A LIBRARY ECOSYSTEM?

Sara Kelly Johns

T he selection of the term "ecosystem" to describe an integrated library network was deliberate. Ecosystems are made up of interrelated and interdependent entities that interact with and depend on each other. In a biological context, an ecosystem is comprised of three fundamental components.[1] First, there is the population comprising all the members of a species that inhabit a given location. Then there is the community, encompassing all the interacting populations of different species in a given area; and then there is the ecosystem itself, the comprehensive ensemble of the entire living community and the physical environment.

Library ecosystems parallel the biological ecosystems in the natural world. Like a biological ecosystem, a library ecosystem is also defined by three fundamental components. First, there is the *population* of all libraries and their workers of all types in a specific geographic location, along with their related supporters. Second, there is the *community* formed by this population along with the patrons who use its libraries: students and families in the general public; primary and secondary schools; colleges and universities; and both governmental and private-sector organizations and institutions. And finally, a *library ecosystem* is formalized by the networking of the libraries, their librarians and library workers, and their supporters, partners, and related organizations.

The American Library Association's Ecosystem Initiative, created to support all libraries, defines the depth and breadth of what can constitute a library ecosystem:

A library ecosystem is the interconnected network of all types of libraries, library workers, volunteers, and associations that provide and facilitate library services for community members; families; K-20 learners; college and university communities; local, state, and federal legislatures and government offices; businesses; nonprofits; and other organizations with specific information needs. A patron of one library is the potential patron of any other library at a different time of life or location. No library exists independent of the library ecosystem.[2]

A Network of Libraries

The are five main types of libraries—public, school, academic, special, and state libraries—and these libraries most often work independently of each other.

Public libraries provide preschool story hours for the youngest children and their parents, strong materials and programming for after-school students, and programming for the interests of the community's youth. Public libraries' collections in all formats, along with classes that support the literacy needs of adult community members, draw in adults in person and electronically.

In elementary, middle, and high schools, school librarians carefully select materials to support students' curriculum and personal interests, coupled with instruction for the developing literacies needed by them. School libraries also often provide safe havens for many. Stories also abound about former students revealing to school librarians that they would not have survived the stress of middle and high school without the school library as a supportive place to spend time.

College and university librarians provide in-depth print and digital collections to support the majors offered in their institutions, reference support, and instruction. All libraries provide a safe place for people to be themselves, connect with others, and learn what they want at their own pace.

Special libraries offer a broad spectrum of industry-focused collections ranging from the law library in the courthouse to the medical library at the hospital, to the archival library in a small town or a university.

State library agencies are part of state and territorial governments and support library services for all state residents. These services include interlibrary loan, reference and research assistance (especially for state archives), public library standards, distribution of Library Services and Technology Act (LSTA) funds, and advocacy for libraries. Most state libraries have open hours for public research and are centers for the distribution of state resources. One example is centralized circulation of resources for the blind and visually impaired.

Libraries thus offer a "cradle-to-grave" continuum of education and support for society. These different types of libraries are interconnected by common goals and by the fact that any library user anywhere might use any of these library types during their lifetime. Every person has access to these libraries, and every community relies on these libraries to support lifelong learning, local businesses, and democratic access to information. Libraries are inherently supportive of our democracy.

Librarians from different library types often cooperate for practical reasons such as sharing access to collections and information about activities. However, the need for a formal ecosystem emerges when libraries are facing controversial issues or when support by library communities is waning or even confrontational. To quote Jim Rettig, a past president of ALA, "If one part of the [library] system is threatened or suffers, the entire system is threatened and suffers."[3]

The additive effect of combining our expertise and experience as a library ecosystem amplifies our experiences and voices. Formalizing a library ecosystem results in *One Voice* where libraries can make a difference together (figure 1.1).

FIGURE 1.1 | **One Voice visualized**

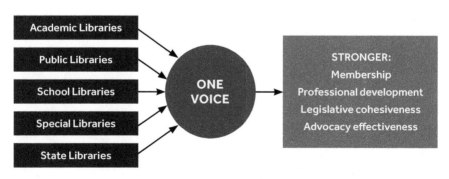

Library Ecosystems: From Localized Communities to National Networks

The library ecosystem's community can expand to involve a municipality or school district that is dealing with budget decisions or with building renovation/expansion approvals. The ecosystem can also extend to a state government facing legislative matters where all types of libraries must collaborate. Furthermore, an ecosystem has the potential for even broader expansion to encompass the entire country or even global communities facing a common issue, such as the censorship of library materials and programs.

Though not necessarily recognized as such, ALA's Unite Against Book Bans initiative is an example of the latter type of ecosystem.[4] It is a national, even global, effort that works as an ecosystem to bring together partners from individual libraries, library associations, foundations, publishers, and many other organizations that support libraries, the arts, and intellectual freedom.

Libraries: Safe Havens and Educational Anchors across the Lifespan

What does ALA's Ecosystem Initiative provide to America's libraries? Library ecosystems can offer a platform for collaborative efforts to promote awareness of the inherent value and universal accessibility of resources to patrons regardless of economic status, race, disability, or ethnicity. Inspiring narratives abound that illustrate how refugees, individuals facing illiteracy, and those with limited education can transform their lives through the diverse resources and programs offered by different types of libraries. The profound impact of cultivating an educated and engaged membership contributes significantly to the betterment of society.

From Diversity to Cohesion:
The Common Ground of Library Values

Each library type has unique services and strengths, but all libraries share core values that define their professional practice. These common values form a solid base that supports all libraries, forming a working ecosystem. Knowing your community and meeting its needs is crucial and can take concentrated and collaborative action by ecosystem members. According to the ALA Ecosystem Continuum:

> At its most effective, the strong library ecosystem supports a diverse library community in speaking with a unified voice about issues that are important to all members of the ecosystem in order to most constructively advance the collective goals of the group.[5]

Every library, regardless of size, whether a small public or school library with just one professional or a large system like the New York City or Seattle public libraries, must engage in marketing and public relations efforts for its promotion. Those two large city libraries on opposite coasts, for example, must create public relations campaigns that reach out to their own communities.

When there are reasons to work collectively with other libraries for the "big picture" support of all libraries, that is when the advocacy provided by an ecosystem is needed. Advocates must consider the collective goal and how all libraries are served well. There is no formula for this, though there are resources that can make it easier. ALA's Ecosystem Toolkit is one such resource.

In the pursuit of creating an advocacy ecosystem, librarians can take a practical step by focusing on user experience (UX) and potentially developing personas that characterize their patron base. Initially, this involves crafting a persona for each library's patron base and then consolidating them collectively. While marketers commonly use personas, colleges and universities also employ them to comprehend how students and faculty use their facilities.

In her description of the User Experience Group at the University of Washington (2009), Jennifer Ward outlined personas that have found utility in various library contexts, including AASL's "National School Li-

brary Standards for Learners, School Librarians, and School Libraries."
Ward and UX experts define personas as "detailed descriptions of imaginary people constructed out of well-understood, highly specified data
about real people."[6]

By examining the overlaps between personas across public, academic, and school libraries in your ecosystem, a targeted approach for collaborative advocacy campaigns can be developed. This tailored strategy
ensures that actions are aligned with the unique needs of stakeholders in
each library type, fostering a unified and impactful advocacy effort.

Defining Advocacy: Contrasts and Commonalities

Beyond the conventional association of advocacy with securing funding
and mandates at local, state, and national legislative levels, an ecosystem
approach can extend the impact of that advocacy. Advocacy not only addresses legislative aspects, but it also fosters public awareness and inspires action. Consider this: How well does the public truly comprehend
the vast scope of what libraries offer and how seamlessly libraries in-
tegrate their services to cater to patrons' needs throughout their lives?
This is the essence of what a library ecosystem delivers. While the public
may grasp this concept in a general sense, collaborative efforts across
diverse library types can serve to deepen the public's understanding of
the profound significance of libraries' services that span all ages and all
sectors of society.

ALA's Committee on Library Advocacy updated ALA's 2009 "Advocacy
Action Workbook" in 2023 as a very practical handbook to plan advocacy
action. The newly updated "Advocacy Action Plan Workbook" includes
steps to build a team for advocacy while considering the axiom that "advocacy is a team sport, bringing together the perspectives and strengths
of multiple players within and, perhaps, beyond your community for
greater reach and impact. The team ensures that advocacy efforts are
on track, tasks are delegated, and communication is ongoing."[7] The Ecosystem Toolkit was developed by a subcommittee of the Committee on
Library Advocacy and complements the updated workbook, offering
methods and tools to strengthen all types of advocacy work through
partnerships, whether for legislative or public awareness.[8]

Every division in ALA has its own definition of library advocacy, as defined by its past and current work and future needs. Examining some of ALA divisions' definitions and approaches shows both similarities and contrasts in their approaches:

- In its Turning the Page advocacy training materials, the Public Library Association (PLA) defines advocacy as "the actions individuals or organizations undertake to influence decision-making at the local, regional, state, national, and international level that help create a desired funding or policy change in support of public libraries."[9] This describes both individual libraries and broader library organizations' public awareness campaigns, from the local to international levels.
- Two ALA divisions, the American Association of School Librarians (AASL) and the Young Adult Library Services Association (YALSA), offer the same definition of library advocacy in their resources: library advocacy is an "ongoing process of building partnerships so that others will act for and with you, turning passive support into educated action for the library program. It begins with a vision and a plan for the library program that is then matched to the agenda and priorities of stakeholders."[10] This definition demonstrates the importance of partnerships between school and youth librarians and reflects these ALA divisions' commitment to providing resources that can be used by school and youth librarians as well as their supporters to demonstrate the value of their work on behalf of children and learning.
- The Association of College and Research Libraries (ACRL) division has a multifaceted approach to legislative advocacy, called ACRL Speaks Out, with the goal of increasing the ACRL's visibility and influence in the arena of higher education policy development, legislation, and best practices.[11] The ACRL has a tightly focused definition for its legislative advocacy, one that does not include individual librarians in their own places of work. However, the ACRL's Academic Library Advocacy Toolkit is a LibGuide with well-curated resources for individual librarians' advocacy when facing challenges in their workplaces.[12]

With all libraries, it is often the perceptions held by the general public and the users of libraries that require public-facing advocacy. Carefully defining the stakeholders, including the decision-makers, for advocacy efforts is a crucial step for success. The definitions given above are examples of library divisions and their members facing outward, an effort that requires focus. The creation of library ecosystems makes the work broader, incorporating supporters and partners that goes beyond librarians and library workers to include organizations and individuals who value the role of libraries in society.

The Four Pillars of an Effective Ecosystem

An effective library ecosystem contains four interrelated pillars. These Ecosystem Continuum pillars serve as supports for a structure that results in *One Voice* that can resonate with decision-makers and policymakers. The four pillars are Leadership, Communication, Collaboration, and Sustainability.[13]

Leadership

We join local, state, or national library organizations to have a strong voice. However, in many states, not all library types stand together in a single association, making it more difficult for them to work together at the state level. Leadership must recognize the need for a library ecosystem and break down the silos to make a difference. Thus, for a library ecosystem, leadership is the first pillar. It takes a few individuals to recognize that advocacy can be more vigorous when all groups work together to make change happen. These leaders begin the ecosystem effort by developing an agenda for the first meeting and reaching out to others to join in the work. These leaders then work to maintain forward momentum.

Communication and Collaboration

Communication and collaboration add strength to advocacy goals and methods. It takes time and commitment to consistently check back with an ecosystem group to ensure that everyone is aware of the objectives and continues supporting the work.

Library ecosystems can be multilayered, possibly beginning with a local group of library institutions working together for local funding or to handle a censorship challenge. Several local ecosystems might build outward to become an ecosystem across the state. In either a crisis or a long-term advocacy campaign, it is more difficult to develop the tools, messaging, and action steps needed without relying on the resources already available to all. On a national level, ALA state chapters work together to strengthen advocacy efforts by providing tools that state ecosystem efforts can adapt and refine for their local work. Library ecosystems can move easily across boundaries to encourage effective communication and collaboration within and beyond member groups.

Sustainability

The idea of continuity is behind this fourth ecosystem pillar. An ecosystem is not a short-term venture. Establishing a collaborative alliance among leaders from different library types for stronger advocacy may happen quickly in response to an immediate need. However, this structure must become enduring to support long-term success. A strong ecosystem will sustain repeated and refocused efforts over many years of collaboration across library types and will take conscious and consistent attention to its sustainability.

Ecosystems Support Existing Library Organizations

A library ecosystem differs from our already existing professional organizations or state library associations. Professional organizations represent the many faces of librarianship, but their very size sometimes makes collaboration and cross-communication unwieldy. The ecosystem concept offers methods to build strong connections across these chasms. "Chasm" may feel like too strong a word, but the press of daily business does lead to a narrow focus even when a broader awareness is needed.

Even in states with long-standing and robust state associations that include all library types, the habits of functioning within library-type silos can sometimes slow collaborative advocacy work. Finding a balance between how things are and how we would like them to be requires innovators to focus more on bridge-building for the future, while other leaders focus on immediate needs. A best-case scenario brings both efforts together, but this takes imagination, time, and consistent effort.

Each library type derives advantages from collaborative advocacy efforts with a primary focus of advocating at a broader level, demonstrating to the world that libraries are an asset worthy of consistent funding. While tangible benefits like interlibrary loans provide clear examples of collaboration that are understandable to the public and legislature, there is a need for a deeper comprehension of the larger picture. This prompts the fundamental question raised earlier: Why is it crucial to recognize, activate, and sustain the library ecosystem? Understanding the contributions of ALA's Ecosystem Initiative to library patrons, communities, and American democracy becomes imperative, underscoring the potential loss to the American experience in its absence.

Advocacy in Action

The New York Library Association (NYLA) holds an annual Advocacy Day at the state capitol in Albany. On that day, librarians, trustees, and library supporters from all types of libraries make appointments with their legislators to discuss the condition of New York State's libraries and the legislative agenda developed by NYLA's legislative committee.

The rally in the Legislative Office Building features speeches by legislators, librarians, and library supporters. I will never forget the legislator who said one year long ago: "If the librarians don't care enough to show up, why should I care about their bills?"

At one exciting Advocacy Day in the capital, school librarians brought student groups with signs and T-shirts promoting the value of strong libraries. The energy reached a new level when the Queens Library buses arrived, filled with patrons who love their libraries. The community of library lovers sent a strong message that day!

When legislators' offices are filled with all types of librarians, along with trustees and members of the public, all of whom are voters in their districts, those legislators pay attention. This is an ecosystem in action with *One Voice*, a loud voice.

With a deeper understanding of what an ecosystem is and the power that ecosystems have, we hope you are ready to work collaboratively and effectively with all librarians and their partners to have the *One Voice* needed to make a difference. Libraries have power; ecosystems have even more.

NOTES

1. New York State Education Department, "The Living Environment Course Syllabus," 2000.
2. American Library Association, "ALA Ecosystem Initiative," www.ala.org/advocacy/ala-ecosystem-initiative.
3. Jim Rettig, "Library Ecosystem at Work," American Library Association, web.archive.org/web/20230706124632/www.ala.org/tools/research/librariesmatter/additup/library-ecosystem.
4. American Library Association, "Unite Against Book Bans," https://unite againstbookbans.org.
5. American Library Association, "Ecosystem Continuum, Definition," www.ala .org/sites/default/files/advocacy/content/Library%20Ecosystem%20 Continuum%20Updated.pdf.
6. Jennifer Ward, "Persona Development and Use, or How to Make Imaginary People Work for You," in Proceedings of the 2010 Library Assessment Conference, pp. 477–93, University of Washington, http://hdl.handle.net/ 1773/19303.
7. American Library Association, Committee on Library Advocacy, "Advocacy Action Plan Workbook," 2023, p. 7, www.ala.org/advocacy/advocacy-action -planning.
8. American Library Association, "Advocacy Action Plan Workbook."
9. Public Library Association, "Turning the Page: Putting Advocacy into Practice," www.publiclibraryadvocacy.org/putting-advocacy-into-practice/.
10. Young Adult Library Services Association, "Advocacy Resources," www.ala .org/yalsa/advocacy; American Association of School Librarians, "What Is Advocacy?" www.ala.org/aasl/advocacy/definitions.
11. Association of College & Research Libraries, "ACRL Speaks Out," www.ala .org/acrl/issues/acrlspeaksout.
12. Association of College & Research Libraries, "Academic Library Advocacy Toolkit," https://acrl.libguides.com/advocacytoolkit.
13. American Library Association, "ONE VOICE: Building a Strong Library Ecosystem," www.ala.org/advocacy/ala-ecosystem-initiative.

2

UNITING AROUND CORE VALUES AND COMMON GOALS

Dorcas Hand

The idea of a library ecosystem is relatively new, but the interdependence of libraries has been true for most of the history of libraries. Libraries have shared books and other materials with other libraries as well as with users. Libraries have collaborated on programming, sharing expenses for author visits and technology tools that no one library can afford alone. Expansive public library systems with branches across urban, suburban, and even rural areas share the revenues allotted by their local government. Public school libraries exist across districts, often with centralized support. University libraries often have "branches" in department buildings across campus or across multiple campuses.

However, an *ecosystem*, as defined in this book, is an interconnected network that exists to pursue certain commonly held goals through collaboration. If we consider libraries as a public good for people from birth throughout life, we can see that communities need library services for preschool infants and children (public), school-age children (school), high school graduates (college, university, and community college), non-academic young adults (public), adults across their lifespan (public and university), and professionals (law, medical, and other special libraries). ALA's Core Values of Librarianship offer a base-level understanding of all the facets of professional library work, all of which figure into ecosystem thinking at every stage and across all library types—school, public, academic, and special. Our goals interact similarly as we all work to enact our visionary values through visible work and concrete, observable products and programs.

Core Values

Given this inherent ecosystem-wide need to understand our common values and goals and collaborate in our efforts to increase public awareness of these, we must ask ourselves, "What are the core values and goals that we see across library types and the geography of our country?" Understanding what all libraries have in common will feed and support our advocacy goals. For this understanding, we look to the Core Values of Librarianship listed by ALA as revised and approved in January 2024. This new list of five values is much easier to remember than the twelve previous ones, but all twelve of those essential concepts remain embedded in the new set. Librarians with MLS degrees have been steeped in these values and will continue to consider them throughout their careers. The five values, "*access, equity, intellectual freedom and privacy, public good, and sustainability*," are ones that most of us can remember as we work. In case any readers are more familiar with the longer list, we provide some insight into how they coalesce into only five because all twelve show up repeatedly in our work across different library types (see figure 2.1).

FIGURE 2.1 | **The library ecosystem and core values**

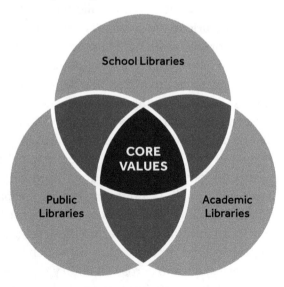

Access

Access provides opportunities for everyone in the community to obtain library resources and services with minimal barriers or disruption. Library workers create systems that ensure that all members of their community can freely access the information and diverse perspectives they need for learning, growth, and empowerment regardless of technology, format, or delivery methods. Access is essential to a vibrant democracy, a culture of ongoing education and lifelong learning. Access includes *social responsibility*, which entails the library staff's awareness of the information needs of their diverse patron community as reflected in library materials' content, format, language, and availability.

Equity

Library workers play a crucial role in fostering equity by actively working to dismantle barriers and create spaces that are accessible, welcoming, and beneficial for all. This is accomplished by recognizing and addressing systemic barriers, biases, and inequalities and creating inclusive library environments where everyone can benefit from the library's offerings and services. Without equity, *access* is weakened and education for all is impossible.

Intellectual Freedom and Privacy

Intellectual freedom empowers people to think for themselves and to make informed decisions while respecting each individual's dignity and independence. Library workers encourage people to cultivate curiosity and form ideas by questioning the world and accessing information from diverse viewpoints and formats without restrictions or censorship. The right to privacy is a crucial safeguard of this freedom, ensuring that everyone has the right to develop their own thoughts and opinions free of surveillance.

Public Good

The public good involves working to improve society and protect the rights to education, literacy, and intellectual freedom. Libraries are an essential public good and are fundamental institutions in democratic societies. Library workers provide the highest service levels to create informed, connected, educated, and empowered communities.

Sustainability

Sustainability means making choices that are good for the environment, that make sense economically, and which treat everyone equitably. Sustainable choices preserve physical and digital resources that reflect community history and interests, as well as keeping services useful now and into the future. By supporting climate resiliency, library workers create thriving communities, care for our common good, and ensure a better tomorrow.

Service and Professionalism

Service is the basis on which all of these core values rely. Professionalism is a key component of service which ensures that the best part of our library training is always the face our public sees. Once the library profession understands all the elements of service that we have in common, we can make these ideas clear to our public more successfully. In short, professionalism and service are embedded in all five of the core values: librarians seek to provide quality service to ensure *access, equity,* and *intellectual freedom and privacy*, which all contribute to the *public good* and the *sustainability* of libraries and communities.

Local Core Values

While the list of core values from ALA is a great starting point, it's also important to look more locally. Many state library groups also list the core values to which they aspire. For example, the following list of core values from the Texas Library Association describes areas essential to the practice of librarianship in every Texas library.

Texas Library Association's Core Organizational Values

- Continuous improvement towards excellence in libraries and librarianship
- Diversity and inclusiveness
- Equity of access to information in a changing environment
- Ethical responsibility and integrity
- Intellectual freedom
- Literacy and lifelong learning
- Social responsibility and the public good

Source: Texas Library Association (TLA), "TLA Core Organizational Values," chart, jpg. 2022. Permission from Shirley Robinson, TLA Executive Director.

Both ALA and the various states' core values remind new ecosystem teams of the commonalities across library types, as well as the tangible impacts these commonalities offer all communities.

Common Goals across Library Types

The Ecosystem Subcommittee developed the following list of goals for our presentations. These are concepts our audiences could easily see in eco-system work because we were working with the older ALA list of twelve values, which was too cumbersome for our programs. In this situation, we needed librarians new to the idea of collaborative advocacy to clearly see that the goals they worked towards every day in their individual libraries were closely aligned with the goals of every other library they might know (see figure 2.2). Their home library goals structure some communication, offer measurable outcomes, and contribute to public perceptions that the library is valuable to the community. In the cross-library type of collabo-rative setting, these goals also facilitate quick understanding and simple explanations to forward libraries' advocacy efforts.

Information literacy speaks to both *democracy* and *diversity*, as well as *access*. All patrons of any age need support to locate correct and current information, access diverse information, and acquire the skills needed to discern the best answers to their questions.

Love of learning is really another way to say *education and lifelong learning*, or *access*. All librarians model a love of learning for their patrons through their ongoing professional continuing education, as well as the programs and resources the library offers the community.

Strong community speaks to the *public good, diversity,* and *social responsibility*. Libraries are open to all and offer books and digital materials to support their patrons' disparate questions and resource needs.

The *historical record* involves *preservation,* or *sustainability*. Whether the library serves a school campus, a neighborhood or city, or a university, one of its goals is to support the preservation of the historical record of that community.

Public access reminds us of the need to welcome all members of the community by offering everyone access to the books and resources they want or need.

Inquiry skills are closely related to information literacy but are more focused on supporting the information-seeking skills needed—skills that librarians teach and support for all patrons.

Intellectual freedom reflects our commitment to offering all patrons access to all the information they seek, even if the librarian may disagree with an opinion. It also includes *confidentiality and privacy* to ensure that patrons can search and view whatever they need.

FIGURE 2.2 | **Common goals across library types: One Voice for library advocacy**

Public Access

Inquiry Skills

Love of Learning

Historical Record

Information Literacy

Strong Community

Source: ALA Ecosystem Initiative, ala.org/advocacy/ala-ecosystem-initiative

Different Kinds of Libraries, Same Mission ————————

We know that all libraries, whether they are school libraries, public libraries in communities, college and university libraries, or even special libraries with a focus on law, medicine, or genealogy, have a culture of learning as a key part of their mission. The patrons who visit every library are interested in learning something new. The library staff is interested in ensuring that the information they find is correct and current. The staff will work to help patrons learn how to evaluate information by analyzing its source, currency, possible bias, and so on. The library works to include all members of the community and ensure access to all the information they seek. Let's consider how these goals and values look in each library type, and how all libraries rely on their collective strengths. Figure 2.3 illustrates how library type and patron age or stage of life interact as factors in library usage and needs.

School Libraries

As figure 2.3 on the following page illustrates, K-12 schools are most students' first exposure to libraries. School libraries give students their first independent opportunity to access books and information chosen for their age and ability, and to use these to support both their personal interests and classroom assignments. Certified school librarians are also teachers, who are familiar with the campus curriculum as well as teachers' needs and personal enthusiasms. Librarians teach every student in the school, every year. The school library inspires a love of learning as it offers a wealth of fiction and nonfiction for all ages and grades in the school. The librarian is there to help students learn how to find, select, and borrow the perfect book or digital resource for today's needs. And teachers are equally supported by the same librarian and the curated collection, so they can expand their curricular lessons with additional resources. Libraries are essential in encouraging literacy, as they offer books that encourage student choice for personal interest, beyond what titles may be required in the classroom.

School librarians teach information literacy and inquiry skills, both how to find information and how to dig into that information so as to determine its usefulness and relevance to the assignment. Students with

FIGURE 2.3 | **The library ecosystem: Key services by library type**

Library Type	Infant/ Preschool	K–12 School	College	Adult
Public	• Storytimes • Sensory play	• Provide additional resources/ reading materials • After-school programs • Summer reading programs	• Provide additional resources/ reading materials	• Meet community-wide needs • Community programs • Business resources • Reading materials
Academic			• Provide resources to support research and coursework • Teach information literacy	• Provide college/ university staff with resources and support
School		• Support curriculum with resources and through co-teaching • Lead dynamic school-wide reading culture • Teach all forms of literacy and digital citizenship; prepare for career and college • Teach and support technology integration		• Collaborate and co-teach with other teachers • Provide specific resources to teachers • Provide professional development • Provide resources to parents

access to a skilled teacher-librarian are well prepared for higher levels of school, and for adult life. They already have information skills and are ready for higher-level access and understanding.

Some students have questions about world events, political happenings, and even history or science topics. The library offers every student access to the answers to whatever questions they have, no matter how sensitive—unless a child's parent has specifically denied the student permission to read certain authors or topics. Barring that parental block, libraries support the intellectual freedom of all students, and the confidentiality of what they borrow or search.

Public Libraries

Public libraries welcome patrons of all ages, from infancy to senior years. High school graduates newly joining the workforce may use the public library system to find career information and job opportunities. As they mature into active citizens, these patrons appreciate recreational reading, topics of ongoing education, and a place for community meetings. As they become parents, the children's room gains primacy—especially preschool storytime, which offers a community space as they meet other new parents, and as they select books for pre-readers to enjoy at home. Entrepreneurs will appreciate a steady source of new ideas, and small business owners will appreciate resources to help them build their businesses. Elementary students and young adults will enjoy the library space and collection during after-school hours and during summer, when the school library is not open. This extended access is important to encourage students to read year-round.

Throughout all these activities, library staff offer full access to all patrons regardless of age or background, while always requesting that parents oversee the children's selections according to their home values. The staff encourage patrons to understand inquiry and information literacy skills. Intellectual freedom remains essential, along with privacy and confidentiality—despite the resource challenges that have become so common recently.

Community College, College, and University Libraries

When high school graduates move through their education towards adulthood, some of them head immediately to jobs, but others enter a community college or a four-year college or university. College and university librarians face many of the same challenges as community college personnel, but they also support students who are in the last years of a four-year undergraduate education or possibly a graduate degree program. All librarians in higher education help students build on the library skills they may have learned in K-12. These students need to understand broader information access and higher levels of research, inquiry, and information literacy. Intellectual freedom, privacy, and confidentiality remain important, and parental oversight is less important as students reach legal maturity.

Special Libraries

Special libraries encompass a variety of specialized libraries that support narrow topics. Law libraries are important components in law schools, but many law firms maintain their own focused legal library in support of their case work. Medical libraries are in medical schools, but also in large hospitals. Genealogy collections support ancestry enthusiasts. There is not a topic that might not have its own library somewhere. Despite the narrow focus of these collections, the underlying goal remains the same: to offer patrons who need this specialized content the access and knowledge base they deserve.

Standing Together on Our Common Values

School, public, and academic librarians interact with one another to ensure the success of all. Advocacy, whether directed towards governmental funding or public awareness, is strongest when all librarians work together. Our communities don't always see the connections that are so clear to us, so we need to make them more obvious by methods of mutual advocacy. When we stand together to speak with *One Voice*, we are more likely to be successful. And in an era when basic democratic principles appear at risk, this strength in numbers is especially important. We want to encourage our patrons to speak with us, to join our strong *One Voice*.

Work across the Ecosystem

So far, we've looked at the various values and goals as interrelated but abstract concepts. Let's take a minute to look at two of them in context, to see them as our librarians and users experience them over time.

A Closer Look at Access

Every library works to ensure that all its patrons have open access to the variety of resources they need to support academic needs and personal interests. K-12 students are curious: they have academic assignments, and they have a steady stream of new interests. Public libraries continue to provide access to information, literacy skills, and constitutional rights. Academic libraries support higher-level coursework that requires broader access to resources in many formats, and coursework in all disciplines that requires students to access more challenging content. As libraries at all levels do their work of offering access to information and encouraging lifelong learning, they remind patrons that libraries are there to support their information needs. We can't really discuss access without mentioning its reliance on the First Amendment rights to read and speak freely, rights that are useless without access to the challenging ideas available in libraries. The Bill of Rights supports the idea of access, and this national document underlies our democracy in every way. Despite our currently polarized communities, we continue to affirm that democracy relies on an informed citizenry, and libraries offer a continuing access point to educate that citizenry.

Building an ecosystem that connects all library types for the benefit of all patrons around the concept of intellectual freedom, as well as other core values, enables ecosystem leaders to unite around a single message spoken with *One Voice* to influence decision-making, public policy, and citizen awareness. Ecosystem participants will need to share a deep understanding of their collective core values, along with the policies—both internal and governmental ones—that undergird an ongoing vibrant library ecosystem that both reflects and contributes to a strong and diverse citizenry of varied opinions, backgrounds, and library needs. We also need to stand strong together against an onslaught of legislation that is currently attempting to undercut the core principles of democracy, especially those of intellectual freedom.

A Closer Look at Sustainability

The sustainability of libraries is usually taken for granted, but as we've seen recently, no library can assume it will remain a welcome element of its community. Let's remember the Patmos Library in western Michigan, which lost its funding in 2022 in two local millage votes over community concerns about LGBT materials offered in the library's collection.[1] We need to constantly renew the public's awareness of the essential role that libraries play in supporting our democracy through our implementation of our core values and our professional service ethic; these reminders are our ongoing advocacy programs. The public needs to understand why we—the ecosystem of libraries—matter to *them*, both individually and as a community throughout their lives. What would the community lose if the library was gone? What assumptions does the public make about access to information that would be invalid should the library not be available to everyone? Public awareness fuels legislative support. Most library supporters are so accustomed to strong libraries that they don't feel a need to speak up when funding comes up for a vote. However, in today's world, we must convince our supporters to be more vocal in the face of a loud minority that works to constrict or defund libraries. Citizens need to join our *One Voice* efforts by speaking out about the importance of libraries. Our libraries will require a strong and vocal support base over the coming years to sustain both a public and legislative understanding of how they contribute to an information-literate and well-informed citizenry; and libraries will continue to require broad support even if the naysayers retreat.

All Together Now

We've looked at the idea of an ecosystem through three lenses: core values, library types, and two specific values, access and sustainability. All libraries are part of an ecosystem whether they recognize it or not. All libraries interact to encourage their diverse population to pursue its own education, and to support American democracy. Regardless of age or income, religious or cultural heritage, language or educational background, all patrons of every age are welcome in libraries and are encouraged by well-educated library staff to locate, understand, and share new ideas. This shows our core values at work in every library every day.

NOTE

1. Ron French, "West Michigan Library Defunded over LGBTQ Books Wins Tax Support 3rd Try," Bridge MI, November 7, 2023, www.bridgemi.com/talent-education/west-michigan-library-defunded-over-lgbtq-books-wins-tax-support-3rd-try.

PART II

Elements of Ecosystem Thinking

UNDERSTANDING THE FOUR PILLARS OF THE CONTINUUM

Dorcas Hand

There is no *one* right way to establish your ecosystem. Every ecosystem team has the opportunity to choose the best place to start and the best path forward. Every path followed is the right path for that team. Every team will modify its own operations over time.

That said, every path chosen will reflect four interconnected elements: Leadership, Communication, Collaboration, and Sustainability. Without these pillars, ecosystem efforts will not reflect the voices of different libraries, library types, and organizations, or encourage collaborative advocacy across the library community. Leadership involves breaking down silos for effective collaboration, and uniting diverse library organizations to create a unified voice. Communication and collaboration enable and strengthen the advocacy goals of library ecosystems, whether at local or broader levels. Sustainability is crucial for the enduring success of the ecosystem and requires continuous attention and commitment to support long-term collaborative efforts. You can measure your ecosystem's performance in each of these categories by means of the Ecosystem Continuum.

The Ecosystem Continuum

The Ecosystem Continuum (referred to as Continuum) is a rubric that allows a group of ecosystem collaborators to decide on a potential structure for their team.[1] The Continuum offers a starting point for new groups, and an ongoing evaluation tool for established efforts. It offers an entry point for groups that are already working in ecosystem ways—whether or not they have already used the term "ecosystem." Each team will look at the Continuum to see where they are now. What are the team's existing strengths? Where would they like to strengthen their methods or capacity? How might they go about deciding where and how to begin?

This rubric allows users to self-evaluate, and thus move ahead more easily to strengthen their efforts. Each topic offers three levels of content: Beginning, Evolving, and Highly Effective.

Beginning refers to a small group that is starting to work towards a statewide library ecosystem.

Evolving refers to a group that is establishing practices across organizations for a statewide ecosystem.

Highly Effective reflects a system and structures that are in place for a thriving and sustainable statewide ecosystem.

As a user scans down the rubric, they can choose the best level in each line to reflect their own current practices. A team may be "highly effective" on some topics and just "beginning" on others—that is the point. The team may already be doing some things well and might identify other areas that would benefit from deeper consideration. Each team will determine how best to use these ideas to build ever-stronger advocacy efforts.

The continuum is divided into four sections, one for each pillar—leadership, communication, collaboration, and sustainability (figure 3.1). And a rubric is provided for each of these four pillars. (See the following section "The Four Pillars of an Effective Ecosystem.") Within each of these rubrics, a few different topics are given consideration. We'll consider the pillars in greater depth below, but here is some frequently used vocabulary:

Ecosystem team—the committee (e.g., advocacy) or task group that is collaborating across library organizations to create or strengthen a mutual support network, or ecosystem initiative.

Participating organization—any statewide or local library organization, and any other entity larger than just "the library," that is participating in some way in the mutual support network.

Decision-makers—individuals with the authority to approve funding and budgets.

Policymakers—individuals with the authority to enact or change legislation or associated rules and regulation.

(There is often, but not always, overlap between the roles of decision-makers and policymakers.)

These four elements—the ecosystem team, participating organizations, and decision-makers and policymakers—make up the totality of the field in which the mutual support network's activities take place (along with the general public, more distantly).

As you consider the rubrics of the continuum, you may find areas you haven't thought about at all, where your team is just "beginning." You will probably also find some areas where you are already "highly effective," and can build on those strengths. And inevitably, there will be areas where you are in the middle and are "evolving" beyond beginner status towards a highly effective one. The point of this rubric is to help your

FIGURE 3.1 | **The four pillars of the continuum**

These four strands are intertwined and, individually, can direct work towards an increasingly effective ecosystem.

 Leadership for building a state-wide library ecosystem is dependent upon an awareness of and active collaboration with various and diverse library partners. Leadership must facilitate connections across library types as the multiplicity of library types is the ecosystem. Leadership refers to the expertise of representatives from participating groups, internationality around building an inclusive model for participation, and the skills participants offer in communication and collaboration towards sustainable ecosystem effort.

 Communication requires clear, intentional sharing both internally and across participating organizations. It builds a unified voice and advances a shared advocacy and legislative agenda that relfects the goals of diverse stakeholders.

 Collaboration towards a unified advocacy and legislative agenda and consistent messaging requires careful and consistent coordination among all participants that reflects the overlapping needs of all the contributing organizations.

 Sustainability of the ecosystem requires equitable access to participatiion as well as ongoing attention to simple and essential aspects of teamwork.

group find its strengths and build going forward. You can start wherever seems obvious to you. But you will definitely need elements of *leadership* to initiate the ecosystem, *communication* to forge relationships, *collaboration* to establish one message that all members can push out with *One Voice*, and *sustainability* to ensure that the ecosystem's structure remains strong for future advocacy projects. The rest is up to you.

The Four Pillars of an Effective Ecosystem

The Leadership Continuum

Exercising *leadership* in building a statewide library ecosystem depends on an awareness of and active collaboration with various and diverse library partners. The leadership must facilitate connections across library types because the multiplicity of library types is the ecosystem. The leadership relies on the expertise of representatives from participating groups, is intentional about building an inclusive model for participation, and depends on the communication and collaboration skills that participants bring in building a sustainable ecosystem. The rubric for leadership is shown in figure 3.2.

Your group members determined that there is a need for an ecosystem effort because together you hope for stronger advocacy. Perhaps something isn't working as well as participants would like in your current relationships across library types, institutions, and organizations. Or maybe you just realized a topic that would bring you together well. The leaders who are working with the ecosystem team want to be change agents whose goal is to build or improve those relationships.

The Communication Continuum

Communication requires clear, intentional sharing both internally and across participating organizations. It builds a unified voice and can advance a shared advocacy and legislative agenda that reflects the goals of diverse stakeholders. The rubric for communication is shown in figure 3.3.

FIGURE 3.2 | **Leadership Rubric**

	Beginning	Evolving	Highly Effective
Ecosystem Perspective	Participating organization leaders: • understand the goals/priorities/importance of a state ecosystem. • begin to engage with related organizations to build an ecosystem. • build support for the ecosystem effort within their respective organizations.	Participating organization leaders: • actively work to understand the perspectives of other organization leaders' roles within the ecosystem. • bring broader understanding back to individual organizations to build stronger support for participation.	Organization leaders: • understand the infrastructures within the state. • know with whom to coordinate both within and beyond the library associations to influence better outcomes. • bring understanding and knowledge to the leadership.
Change Agent	• Leader-representatives from participating organizations demonstrate responsibility for developing an ecosystem that honors all voices. • Ecosystem leaders convey to participating organizations the benefits of a state ecosystem.	• Leaders take personal responsibility to represent their individual organizations, to honor all voices within the community, and to implement a state ecosystem. • Ecosystem leaders develop regular methods of demonstrating to their organizations the value of the ecosystem.	• Leaders take collective responsibility for maintaining a state ecosystem that reflects all stakeholders within the community. • Ecosystem leaders demonstrate to their organizations the value of the ecosystem through visible, consistent contact with participating organizations.
Core Values	• Leaders understand that ALA's Core Values of Librarianship apply to all libraries.	• Leaders consistently seek to build stronger understanding among Ecosystem participants of ALA's Core Values of Librarianship as they apply across library types.	• Leaders apply deep understanding of ALA's Core Values of Librarianship in the collaborative development of Ecosystem agenda's priorities.
Relationships	• Leaders informally support opportunities to communicate/plan/work towards a state ecosystem. • Leaders develop relationships to support collaborative work.	• Leaders consistently support opportunities to communicate/plan/work together across organizations (advocacy committees, etc.). • Ecosystem leaders share collaborative discussions with organization leadership to maintain strong relationship.	• Leaders informally support opportunities to communicate/plan/work towards a state ecosystem. • Leaders develop relationships to support collaborative work.

FIGURE 3.3 | **Communication Rubric**

	Beginning	Evolving	Highly Effective
Building Communication	• Initial representatives know that one another exists and begin to reach out to representatives of other library organizations. • Initial representatives work to expand representation among other library-related organizations. • Initial representatives explain to the leadership of their participating organizations the idea of this incipient ecosystem effort.	• Representatives of participating organizations have contact information for one another and communicate periodically. • Representatives keep leadership of participating organizations aware of growing communication/collaboration within the ecosystem effort, and request support and input.	• Representatives of participating organizations communicate on a regular basis. • Representatives share with their respective organizations new knowledge and understandings that better support collaborative and inclusive advocacy.
Communication Methods	• Initial representatives begin to develop a communications system to ensure that all interested participants are consistently included in planning and discussions. • Representatives depend on participating organizations' websites for access to current issues, goals, needs of potentially participating organizations. • Representatives utilize membership communication channels available within participating organizations to spread the word about ecosystem efforts.	• Representatives develop regular meetings, whether in person or virtual, to move ecosystem agenda items forward. • Representatives report regularly (at least annually) to the Boards of the participating organizations. • Representatives encourage reciprocal methods—such as sharing meeting minutes or talking points—to share regularly with leadership of participating organizations.	• Representatives participate in frequent open, collaborative meetings (virtual or in person) and information sharing. Representatives engage regularly with their individual organizations' leadership for updated insights throughout the year, to ensure alignment of work. • Representatives utilize consistent reciprocal methods—such as sharing meeting minutes or talking points—to communicate regularly with organization leadership, and to inform the full membership.

	Beginning	Evolving	Highly Effective
Awareness of Contacts	• Initial representatives, working with their respective organizations' committees and leadership, develop awareness of key policymakers and decision-makers across organizations. • Initial representatives will also share these names with the leadership of their individual organizations. • Initial representatives coordinate and explain how libraries are an ecosystem, even before there is an established ecosystem agenda.	• Representatives support participating organization leadership in strengthening and maintaining relationships that are key to implementation of the ecosystem effort and the shared advocacy agenda. • Representatives, working with their respective organizations' committees and leaders, expand and maintain a growing list of policy- and decision-makers who support library issues; the list will be updated at least annually. • Representatives and organization leadership develop methods to build and expand	• Representatives, working with committees and leadership, maintain relationships with library leaders and external influencers who help communicate the value of libraries to the public and to policy- and decision-makers. • Representatives and organization leadership collaborate to maintain and refine methods to ensure consistent and strategic contact with decision-makers and policymakers.
Cooperative Crisis Support	• Representatives keep partners aware of any crises in their individual organizations to facilitate a coordinated response from the ecosystem team. • Representatives share with their participating organization leadership any crisis impacting other participating organizations	• The ecosystem team engages around any crises affecting participating organizations, developing a response plan that might include use of shared tools. • Representatives work with their participating organization leadership to support and further enhance any calls to action within their own communities.	• The ecosystem team works with leadership to organize and coordinate the most useful response in support of crisis solutions for participating library organizations. • The ecosystem team solicits from participating organizations agreed support, which may include coordinated action on behalf of each other.

continued on next page

FIGURE 3.3 | **Communication Rubric (*cont'd*)**

	Beginning	Evolving	Highly Effective
One Voice	• Initial representatives work to develop an equitable and inclusive library ecosystem plan that supports and reflects all potentially participating organizations and the diversity of their memberships. • Initial representatives institute use of consistent, jargon-free vocabulary that will be clear to external audiences. • Representatives consult with appropriate committees and leadership of participating organizations about issues identified for collaborative action and talking points that can be used widely to support ecosystem efforts. • Representatives spread awareness of a shared vocabulary so that all stakeholders can understand the ecosystem agenda when it is published	• Representatives communicate regularly with their respective organizations to ensure everyone remains aware of issues and needs across all participating organizations and their diverse memberships. • The ecosystem team develops messaging using consistent vocabulary to all participating individual organizations as agendas are honed. • The ecosystem team looks for intersections of goals and issues where the participating organizations can work together. • The ecosystem team uses consistent vocabulary (no jargon) with all participating organizations to disseminate the agenda once decided. • Representatives explain that using single voice/message will strengthen the effort, and potential impact. • Representatives also share with their individual organizations the intersections of goals and priorities to strengthen the ecosystem's collective position.	• The ecosystem team and respective organizations speak with *One Voice* advancing a shared agenda. • The shared agenda reflects the needs and goals of all participating organizations and their diverse memberships. • The ecosystem team demonstrates to participating organizations how speaking with One Voice will strengthen the impact of the ecosystem effort. • Working with leadership, representatives develop shared communications and other documentation for use by all participating organizations.

Throughout all your ecosystem efforts, communication will be directed *internally* to the leaders or members as they build their mutual understanding of ecosystem goals. It will also need to be directed *externally* back to the participating organizations to ensure ongoing understanding of and buy-in to ecosystem plans. These discussions will need to be explained to the organizations which the leader-members represent. There will be a constant flow of information working to ensure the enthusiastic support of final choices, as these decisions will inevitably include compromises. The ecosystem team is working to achieve the greatest possibility of success, by sharing and disseminating information to the participating organizations. In any given advocacy agenda, every participant will embrace collaborative goals that reflect the needs of the entire team.

Whatever communication means are employed—and this will probably include a variety of tools—all leader-members will be included internally, and all organizational members are represented equally. All member organizations will consistently be kept informed of the discussion and implementation of the agenda.

It will be important as you develop your communication systems to always remain aware of how different library types overlap in their mission and functions, while at the same time you remember what these nuanced differences actually mean to the libraries' patrons. This awareness will support implementation of the strongest possible advocacy agenda as your team builds one. The Ecosystem Toolkit includes a "Comparison of Public, School and Academic Libraries" (see appendix C in this book), a table that offers a summary of the different missions, visions, and patron groups of the three main types of libraries. This quick-reference tool will support your team members as their understanding of one another grows.[2]

As the ecosystem team gets rolling on their project, they will want to develop a collaborative list of contacts (e.g., chairs of legislative committees, local advocates, etc.) who can potentially help the success of the project. It may seem obvious to say, but the team needs a centralized storage system for lists of names and other information. This information needs to be equally available to the entire team and updated regularly, as specific people in important roles will likely change over time.

The Collaboration Continuum

Collaboration in a unified advocacy and legislative agenda requires consistent messaging and careful and consistent coordination among all participants, to reflect the overlapping needs of all the contributing organizations. The rubric for collaboration is shown in figure 3.4.

Sharing between organizations means your members will work to develop an increasing understanding of their mutual needs. They will want to understand both what is the same, and what is different between their

FIGURE 3.4 | **Collaboration Rubric**

	Beginning	Evolving	Highly Effective
Sharing between Organizations	• As individuals in various library organizations recognize the need to collaborate beyond their organization, they begin to connect across library types and discuss their priorities. • Representatives share back to leadership of participating organizations new understandings of ecosystem interrelationships and priorities.	• Representatives from different library types convene ongoing discussions to shared priorities and build awareness of commonalities across the ecosystem. • Representatives collaborate to propose share messaging to take back to their individual organizations. • Ecosystem representatives develop systems to regularly share with leadership of participating organizations new understandings of ecosystem interrelationships and priorities.	• Representatives of participating organizations extend their understanding of shared priorities and develop ecosystem agendas that interweave the priorities of all for a solid platform that reflects the needs and goals across the ecosystem. • Ecosystem representatives maintain systems to regularly share back to leadership of participating organizations new collaborative understandings of ecosystem interrelationships and priorities. • Library organizations support a climate of direct and regular collaboration.

needs. Over time and with consistent communication, they will build prioritized agendas that are achievable and reflect the needs of all. Each team member will need to be able to explain and hear the nuances as they continue the work. Vocabulary can also be important. The same term can be used differently in different library systems, so agreeing in a specific ecosystem on an inclusive definition of certain potentially confusing terms will be essential to long-term success.

Building a collaborative agenda and priorities requires member representatives to consult with their own organization's leadership in

FIGURE 3.4 | **Collaboration Rubric (*cont'd*)**

	Beginning	Evolving	Highly Effective
Collaborative Agenda and Priorities	• Initial representatives review priorities from each participating organization to compile the annual ecosystem agenda. • Representatives share with leadership of participating organizations an overview list of advocacy priorities, to build awareness of the whole ecosystem and illustrate the breadth and inclusivity of ecosystem discussions.	• Representatives hone from lists of priorities brought from participating organizations an agenda that forwards the agreed mutual goals of the ecosystem. • Representatives share with leadership of participating organizations details of the full list under discussion. • Representatives share the developing ecosystem agenda that focuses on the mutually agreed priorities of most benefit to participating organizations.	• Representatives jointly build the annual agenda to best move forward the agreed mutual priorities of all. • Representatives are transparent with process and encourage ongoing communication and input. • Final prioritized agenda is shared with all participating organizations' leadership and membership.
ALA Connections	• Volunteers and representatives request information to support a new ecosystem effort from state associations and ALA. • Representatives share useful connections and resources with their respective organizations.	• Representatives reach out to state associations, ALA, and ecosystem leaders in other states for ideas and suggestions. • Representatives share useful connections and resources with participating organizations.	• Representatives maintain contact with ecosystem leaders through the state associations and ALA. • Representatives and organization leadership establish opportunities to share information and resources from around the country.

continued on next page

FIGURE 3.4 | **Collaboration Rubric** (*cont'd*)

	Beginning	Evolving	Highly Effective
Advocacy and Legislative	• Initial representatives from participating organizations share advocacy and legislative agenda ideas, needs, and priorities with the group to begin to build a collaborative agenda. • Representatives share preliminary and developing advocacy and legislative agendas with leadership of participating organizations. • All participating organizations begin to share these collaborative efforts to the public and with policymakers to develop broader support for the library ecosystem, as well as for specific agenda priorities.	• Representatives support collaborative goals by sharing new advocacy and legislative issues and priorities as they develop, working together to incorporate these new goals into any existing or developing advocacy agenda. • Representatives encourage their organizations' leadership to follow discussions and contribute suggestions towards robust shared advocacy and legislative agendas. • In coordination with the participating organization leadership and appropriate committees, the ecosystem team helps share information about the library ecosystem and agenda with the public and policymakers.	• Representatives collaborate to build and maintain a current advocacy and legislative agenda that reflects shared priorities and a unified voice. • Representatives check in with leadership and membership of their participating organizations for feedback, support, and continuous development of robust shared advocacy and legislative agendas. • The ecosystem team supports and/or assists with development of public-facing resources to explain the shared agenda in ways the public can easily support.
Events and Resources	• Members of participating organizations attend and participate (e.g., presenter, panelist, etc.) in other organizations' events, such as conferences. • Representatives team to share awareness of resources available to participating organizations to support a collaborative agenda. • Representatives work to reflect back to participating organization leadership the need to provide overlapping events and resources.	• Participating organizations consider representation in planning and production of and attendance at each other's events. • Representatives discuss sharing costs associated with collaborative resources, like a lobbyist. • Representatives encourage participating organizations to develop opportunities for collaborative participation at joint events and with ecosystem-wide resources.	• Participating organizations are represented in planning and production of each other's events or co-host events. • Representatives identify together the best resources to accomplish shared priorities. • Representatives contribute to the planning of joint events of participating organizations and in the development of resources useful to all participating organizations.

developing their own list of advocacy needs that will be contributed to the greater effort. When these several agendas (however many member organizations are joining) are laid out in parallel, the team can begin to see where there is overlap or commonalities between them. This overlap is an easy place to begin the collaborative agenda. The Ecosystem Toolkit offers several "Agenda Building Templates" (see appendix A), which are templates to facilitate this kind of thinking.[3]

As you look at the paralleled agendas of the member organizations, you will likely notice that some organizations are more focused on legislative advocacy, while others are hoping to raise public awareness. Both of these goals are important, but they may be handled separately and differently—even by the same ecosystem team. As a team focuses its agenda, it will be important to differentiate these two goals. Often legislative advocacy relies on public awareness, especially if the legislative goal requires that voting citizens speak up in support of your agenda. They will only speak up if you have raised their awareness of the issue. Nevertheless, the methods that inspire public support are not necessarily the same as those that support legislative success.

Lastly, the members of the ecosystem team can enhance the events and resources initiated by other members. They can both advertise and attend author events, community speakers, and so on. They can also contribute to resource lists that support the community needs of other library types than their own. These efforts are more on the level of concrete collaboration, and thus are not exactly the focus of ecosystem efforts, but they remain potential side effects of stronger connections and cooperative understanding across library types, organizations, and associations. And these concrete bonds do enhance the political awareness of libraries as One Community with *One Voice*.

The Sustainability Continuum

The *sustainability* of the ecosystem requires equitable access to participation in it, as well as ongoing attention to simple and essential aspects of teamwork. The rubric for sustainability is shown in figure 3.5.

With the first three pillars—leadership, communication, and collaboration—you can build a strong ecosystem for immediate purposes and achieve success in your initial goals. But you will probably begin to see

FIGURE 3.5 | **Sustainability Rubric**

	Beginning	Evolving	Highly Effective
Organizational Representation Guidelines	• Initial representatives reach out to partners with a goal of full engagement by all potentially participating organizations. • Representatives emphasize benefits of consistent membership to participating organization leadership and memberships.	• The ecosystem team establishes practices that support ongoing engagement of all participating organizations. • Practices are shared with the leadership of all participating organizations for approval. • Representatives demonstrate the benefits of consistent representation on the ecosystem team and encourage practices that support or require representation.	• The ecosystem team maintains representative membership according to established policies to ensure that all organizations remain fully engaged. • Representatives remain in regular communication with respective organization leadership to reinforce the benefits of consistent representation, and to ensure a timely and seamless transition for new appointees.
Term Overlap	• Initial representatives work to stagger rotation off of ecosystem team and encourage new representation. • Representatives encourage understanding of the need for consistent membership, staggered terms, and new participants.	• Initial representatives work to stagger rotation off of ecosystem team and encourage new representation. • Representatives encourage understanding of the need for consistent membership, staggered terms, and new participants.	• The ecosystem team maintains policies for term overlap and participating organizations maintain supporting policies. • Representatives facilitate the transition of terms, working with their organization's leadership.
Defining the Explicit Representation of Participating Organizations	• Representatives initiate conversation about who needs to be at the library ecosystem table and propose group composition. • Participating organizations recognize and approve representatives to ecosystem effort.	• Organizations recognize ecosystem team as an official collaboration, centered on the best benefit to member groups. • Participating organizations commit to maintaining a representative on the ecosystem team.	• Members of the ecosystem team convene regularly as official representatives of their respective organizations, with an explicit charge to collaborate for the benefit of all member groups. • All state-level library organizations are represented.

	Beginning	Evolving	Highly Effective
Succession Planning	• Representatives are aware of the need to mentor and cultivate new representatives. • Representatives lay groundwork with participating organizations to cultivate a pipeline of ecosystem team participants.	• Representatives work with participating organizations to ensure others are engaged, knowledgeable, and prepared to step into the ecosystem team on schedule. • Representatives work with participating organizations to onboard and train new representatives to the ecosystem who are engaged in and knowledgeable of advocacy and legislative issues. • Representatives emphasize the need for diverse perspectives and new ideas.	• Participating organizations establish a pipeline for volunteers to step into the ecosystem role engaged, knowledgeable, and prepared. • Organization leadership prioritizes mentoring for ecosystem awareness. • Outgoing representatives work consistently with respective organizations to train successors who are engaged in and knowledgeable of advocacy and legislative issues. • Ecosystem representatives build institutional awareness of the benefits of an ongoing ecosystem effort sustained by diverse perspectives and new ideas.
Organizational Relationships	• Initial representatives consider how best to develop open communications between and among all member groups through their designated representatives to this team. • Initial representatives ensure that leadership of participating organizations are sent information about ongoing discussions and recommendations of the ecosystem group.	• Representatives establish regular systems to engage with their individual organizations, sharing ongoing plans and receiving feedback on new topics for agenda development. • Representatives develop a system to receive from participating organizations an annual list of advocacy priorities to facilitate the team's work.	• Representatives maintain ongoing systems to engage with their organizations, sharing ongoing plans and receiving feedback on new topics for agenda development. • Representatives maintain systematic communication with the leadership of the participating organizations.

continued on next page

FIGURE 3.5 | **Sustainability Rubric (*cont'd*)**

	Beginning	Evolving	Highly Effective
Ecosystem Calendar	• Initial representatives begin to document important dates and any recurring cycles that impact ecosystem function. • Initial representatives build a team agenda that anticipates cyclic deadlines in order to accommodate appropriate action. • Representatives share the ecosystem calendar with all participating organizations to increase understanding of the ecosystem team activities.	• Representatives keep ecosystem calendar updated, adding information that will support agenda-building or implementation. • Representatives share the ecosystem calendar with all participating organizations to increase understanding of the ecosystem team activities.	• Representatives integrate ecosystem calendar with organizations' calendars. • Representatives spread awareness of the implementation schedule to extend understanding of the ecosystem team impact.
Team Continuous Improvement Plan	• Representatives discuss past actions to identify what worked, what didn't, and what future success will look like.	• Representatives review ecosystem work after any milestone date (final advocacy agenda item, legislative success, etc.), in order to seed new ideas for methods and/or content. • Representatives solicit feedback from organization leadership to ensure that the ecosystem efforts remain aligned with and beneficial to all participating organizations. • Representatives share with the leadership of participating organizations reflections on progress and areas in need of improvement.	• Representatives establish an annual review process to evaluate work and goal-setting methods. Concrete successes and failures reviewed as a way to seed new ideas for methods and/or content, and to demonstrate transparency. • Leadership is surveyed annually as part of the evaluation process; questions include successes, challenges, ideas, and recommendations for the future. • Representatives share with leadership and members of participating organizations the continuous improvement plan.

additional projects that are ripe for ecosystem attention. So how can you make your ecosystem sustainable over time?

In order to continue to engage all the member organizations, you will want to establish clear policies for membership, and for representative turnover. The word "membership" refers here to a participating organization, while "representative" refers to the designated person from that organization sitting on the ecosystem team. There may be additional organizations that want to join, and that can bring great ideas and energy to the effort.

You will want to ensure that not every representative rotates out of the team at the same time, so some version of term overlap will be important.

You will need to explicitly define representation: What does it mean? What are a representative's duties? What are the benefits? Governance documents seem tedious until they are needed but writing them well at the beginning can go far to ensuring a sustainable group effort.

Your hope is that the member organizations will remain enthusiastic about continuing to participate in the ecosystem team. Their enthusiasm really depends on your successful implementation of strong communication back to the member organizations' leadership, communication that inspires them to see how libraries are truly stronger together. Enthusiastic member organizations will make sure they have a new representative chosen, who is ready to step up and join the team when it is time. This is what is called effective "succession planning."

Sustainability also requires ongoing attention to the relationships between the member organizations. The representatives sitting together at one table is the easy part. Building positive relationships among organizations or institutions that may not have been cooperative in the past takes attention.

Look to Existing Organizational Models

There is a reason why these steps remind you of how ALA and other library organizations work. Large organizations in many fields have learned over time that if every leader leaves at the same time, there is mass confusion in trying to move the project forward. They have also learned that every unit, from the executive board to small committees, needs a breadth of knowledge and experience to be successful in its charge. It makes sense to use good models for this new focus.

Ecosystem efforts require time and persistent attention. Members must decide the actual agenda and priorities. Then they must draft the message, and train everyone how to communicate this message with *One Voice*. And then they must speak with that *One Voice* to push the message out, and watch it work (or occasionally not). Possibly, the message will have to be adjusted. And finally, there is evaluation. Why list all these stages? Because time management is key, and a planning calendar will be important. Since much of this work may be focused on the legislative calendar of your state or local government, your own calendar may revolve on when they are likely to vote on your item, and then you must work backwards from that date to get all of your ecosystem work accomplished in time.

You probably evaluate your library projects as they are completed. This will be important for the ecosystem team as well. The member organizations will appreciate regular reports on progress, as well as on success and needed improvements. Continuous improvement is always a goal.

Lastly, you will need to find ways to work with dissension. Perhaps one member representative is working to convince their organization to accept a compromise, but their effort is not going well. How can the team support that representative's efforts? Dissension is a fact of life, and building compromise is never easy. But a successful ecosystem team will need to address these issues. Robert's Rules of Order are a fallback used by many groups, but you may choose a different method. It is your group.

If at First You Don't Succeed

Ecosystem work is an iterative effort. You may not succeed on the first try, but that doesn't mean the ecosystem has failed. It means you have more work to do within the same ground rules. Teachers know that the first time an idea is introduced, the students barely hear it; the second time they may realize they've heard it before; by the third time, they begin to realize that this idea is important to understand, and it might even be on the test! An ecosystem initiative will keep reintroducing the best ideas, perhaps with new language or examples, but always reminding the broader audience of their consistent importance.

The more ecosystem team members understand and honor the needs of their team colleagues and the parent organizations, the more successful the overall effort is likely to be because that agenda will be based on the strongest possible understanding of the mutual needs of all participants.

Adapt the Continuum to Your Needs

"One Voice: A Continuum for Stronger Library Ecosystems" is a tool for library advocates at all levels to use. Advocacy efforts across the United States, whether local, state, regional, or within ALA, can adapt the continuum and its associated tools to build robust ecosystem efforts and achieve short-term advocacy success. They can also put in place an infrastructure that supports ongoing advocacy efforts across library types, organizations, and institutions over the longer term. The four pillars of Leadership, Communication, Collaboration, and Sustainability can facilitate stronger existing advocacy efforts as well as support new groups, especially in combination with the rubric structure of Beginning, Evolving, and Highly Effective. This systemic effort to maintain a body that understands the sometimes-conflicting needs of its partners is not easy, but the results can be hugely effective. A living library ecosystem is much stronger than any of its component partners can be alone. The communication and collaborative compromises you make together contribute to a stronger result. And the team you build can morph as needed over time to remain a powerful force for library advocacy.

NOTES

1. American Library Association, "One Voice: A Continuum for Stronger Library Ecosystems," www.ala.org/sites/default/files/advocacy/content/Library%20Ecosystem%20Continuum%20Updated.pdf.
2. American Library Association, "A Comparison of Public, School, and Academic Libraries: Vital to Our Communities," www.ala.org/sites/default/files/advocacy/content/Ecosystem%20Public%2C%20School%20and%20Academic%20Libraries%20Fact%20Sheet_0.pdf.

3. American Library Association, "Ecosystem Agenda Building: Information Gathering: Template for Building a Collaborative Advocacy Agenda," One Voice, www.ala.org/sites/default/files/advocacy/content/stateandlocal/Ecosystem/Ecosystem%20Agenda%20Building%20Template%20-%20Information%20Gathering.docx.pdf.

ECOSYSTEM LEADERSHIP
Beginning, Building, and Sustaining

Michelle Robertson

f you aspire to create an ecosystem initiative or fortify an existing one that is dedicated to advocating for the comprehensive needs of librarians, consider stepping into the role of a library ecosystem leader. The leaders of such an initiative share a common vision for a strong collaborative library advocacy effort with a team who have joined together to accomplish their shared vision. Being an ecosystem leader involves making decisions, communicating effectively, and collaborating to provide direction and support to a team of advocates and their group of librarians and their supporters. A leader motivates and empowers others to achieve success, and also manages both people and resources effectively. But first, being an ecosystem leader requires the vision to see how ecosystem thinking can strengthen library advocacy; it does not necessarily mean that you are already in an official leadership position in either a library or a library advocacy organization.

An ecosystem initiative can be started by as few as two leaders who see the need to build stronger advocacy for the libraries around them. They can become leaders by acting on their shared vision and inviting other interested advocates to join them. They can bring their library organization on board—an advocacy initiative does not operate independently of the libraries it is advocating for.

Let's look at what leadership means in the context of ecosystem ideas.

Characteristics of a Leader

There are many qualities that can make someone a good leader. Some important qualities pertinent to the role of an ecosystem leader include:

1. *Vision*: A good leader should be able to articulate a clear and compelling vision for the future that inspires and motivates others.
2. *Integrity*: Leaders should be honest, ethical, and have a strong sense of honor. They should be trusted by their followers and lead by example.
3. *Communication skills*: Good leaders should be able to communicate effectively, both in writing and verbally. They should be able to listen to others and respond clearly and concisely.
4. *Flexibility*: A good leader should be able to adapt to changing circumstances and be open to new ideas and approaches.
5. *Empathy*: Leaders should be able to understand and relate to the feelings and perspectives of others. They should be able to put themselves in other people's shoes to consider their needs and concerns.
6. *Determination*: Good leaders will need to make decisions quickly and confidently, even in difficult or uncertain situations.
7. *Resilience*: Good leaders should be able to bounce back from setbacks and failures, maintain a positive attitude in the face of adversity, and be ready to regroup and try again.

These are just some of the characteristics of a good leader. Different situations may require different leadership styles and approaches; a good leader should be able to adapt their style to fit the needs of their team and organization.

Shared and Changing Leadership

Leadership is a continuous process and requires ongoing communication, collaboration, and adaptability to changing circumstances. As an ecosystem team works together at different points in time, the leaders might be different individuals based on their skill set. An ecosystem does not consist of just one person or one leader; it is comprised of several individuals who share the leadership role to accomplish the initiative's vision and goals. In the context of an ecosystem, leadership draws upon "the expertise of representatives from participating groups, intentionality around building an inclusive model for participation, and the skills participants offer in communication and collaboration towards a sustainable ecosystem."[1]

Leading the Change: Vital Concepts for Ecosystem Success

Leaders are essential for creating a cohesive ecosystem. They provide direction, inspiration, accountability, and relationship-building skills that help drive their group of library advocates toward success in their endeavors to support all libraries. No matter whether you are a beginning leader, an evolving one, or a highly effective leader, there is a role for you in an ecosystem.

An Ecosystem Perspective

Beginning leaders understand a lot of what is happening within the ecosystem but are not at the point of guiding the conversation and helping to set goals.

Evolving leaders actively seek to listen to other individuals' perspectives on key library issues. They work towards finding a middle ground that all members can understand and support.

Highly effective leaders understand the organizational structure of the different key groups; they know who to reach out to within their organization and beyond when it comes time to collaborate for the greater good of libraries; and they share their knowledge with other leaders in different organizations.

Change Agents

A "change agent" in an organization is an individual or a group who takes the first steps to create change. All success stories start with someone or a group taking those first few tentative steps to create an ecosystem of advocates for all libraries.

Beginning leaders can communicate with others the significance of an ecosystem and can communicate the need to create an ecosystem that will represent all librarians.

Evolving leaders can implement an ecosystem that represents all voices and will demonstrate the strength of an ecosystem on a regular basis.

Highly effective leaders are responsible for maintaining the ecosystem and demonstrating on a regular basis the value of the ecosystem.

Collaboration

The team of leaders in an ecosystem collaborate to build relationships both within and outside of the organization that will support the mission of the initiative.

Beginning leaders support the development of an ecosystem and the opportunities to collaborate and plan for an ecosystem.

Evolving leaders actively support collaboration and work towards an active ecosystem.

Highly effective leaders provide a wide variety of opportunities for the new ecosystem members and library types to collaborate-and work together to create a collaborative agenda.

Communication

To create a strong ecosystem, the leadership team will need to lead by using collaboration and communication. A leader or the leadership team needs to be aware of the common goals that will support all librarians. Team leaders should articulate a clear and complete vision of the advocacy needs the initiative is hoping to address; these can evolve into the ecosystem goals. These leaders will guide the group to set specific goals and objectives that align with supporting all library types with *One Voice*. The leadership team will communicate on a regular basis with the committee of representatives to keep everyone informed of progress towards the common goal and on track with their assignments towards that goal. This communication should be two-way, listening actively to the ideas and concerns of the group's members while encouraging collaboration among the team members to foster an environment where everyone feels valued and included.

When an initiative's leadership follows these strategies, they can effectively lead their committee of representatives towards a common goal and help them achieve success.

Focus Your Ecosystem Around Common Goals

Consider these common-ground topics when setting your ecosystem goals:

- *Equity of access* is a topic that can bring all types of librarians to the table and help create an ecosystem. All librarians view their libraries as places that welcome everyone and aim to provide access to materials for all their patrons.
- *Information literacy* and *the right to read* are also focal points for all librarians. We support the right of everyone to have the kinds of books they want to read and to obtain information on any subject they desire.

Next Steps

Find colleagues who are also interested in improving advocacy efforts and who will work with you to create your ecosystem. Your ecosystem might be limited to your specific library type or to your county—or it might extend across your entire state. Starting small and taking those first few steps will help you feel more confident as you work towards creating a statewide library ecosystem. If you already have an advocacy committee within your state library association, start talking about how ecosystem thinking can increase the impact of your advocacy efforts.

Congratulations! You are a leader, whether you knew it or not. You stepped up with the vision to begin a library ecosystem that will strengthen advocacy for its library members and others. Now the real fun begins as you see how to make the action happen, how to enact advocacy across your ecosystem.

NOTE

1. Lisa Wells, Ecosystem Interview with Michelle Robertson, August 2023.

PROGRESS REQUIRES STRONG COMMUNICATION

Eryn Duffee

C ommunication is key to establishing and sustaining any ecosystem initiative. In today's world, not only does communication have to be multipronged, but it must also be active. It is not enough to reach a consensus among the active members of a library organization. It is not enough to state that consensus on a stagnant website. And it is not enough to rely on a lobbyist to state your position to legislatures (should you be so lucky to have one).

Every piece of communication to potential advocacy partners should include two crucial parts. First, share the *why*. Why is this a worthy cause? Why is this relevant?? Then, share the call to action. What can I do about it at this moment? How can I find out more information? How do I stay involved?

Even the most brilliant idea means nothing if it cannot be communicated effectively. Likewise, you could have the support of every person in an ecosystem for a cause and never move the needle an inch if no one knows who is on board and where the ship is heading. Therefore, communication by members back to their collaborative organizations, towards the public, and with policymakers must be consistent and vigorous.

Utilizing All Avenues for Effective Communication ———

Advocacy communication within the ecosystem should be bidirectional. Leadership and the representatives of participating organizations should survey the membership about their advocacy goals and how such goals could be achieved. This data will support the ecosystem work. Also, this bidirectional communication will bring fresh ideas to the ecosystem effort and increase buy-in and participation from the represented organizations. Holding webinars, open meetings, and advocacy-focused conferences will effectively maintain those communication channels in public forums and offer transparency to the broader community.

When rallying support and informing your membership of an initiative, it is essential to reach people where they get their information and in a method that is consistent with that format. For example, short social media posts with an important message and a shortened URL or hashtag (figure 5.1), combined with longer e-mail newsletter segments, will reach more people. Having both these forms redirect to a website with all the necessary information, links to relevant articles, and a call to action will garner more engagement and allow your members to answer questions and share information more easily.

FIGURE 5.1 | **Washington Library Association social media post**

Washington Library Association
School Library Division

Town Hall
Meeting

Objectives:
• Increase participation in advocacy efforts for School Library Programs
• To share steps that you could do locally to help build advocacy across the state

WEDNESDAY
AUGUST 16, 9AM

MEET US HERE!
https://tinyurl.com/ckzye4vm

If actively utilized, online members-only communities are another effective form of digital communication. Communication leaders should keep an eye on the horizon for these, as more effective tools are routinely being created and implemented.

Conferences, in addition to providing professional development and hosting in-person committee meetings, can create that "mountaintop experience" that inspires attendees to engage more in advocacy and professional work throughout the year. Moreover, the participants make social connections that can foster more profound work toward the common cause. Such gatherings also facilitate sharing information and skills long after the projector screens have come down. Keynotes and welcoming addresses can inform the attendees about upcoming advocacy efforts, ways to engage, and current challenges that need to be addressed through action and advocacy.

Webinars and virtual events are the new normal in our post-pandemic world. Incorporating advocacy messages into "virtual conference"-style events can help reach a larger audience. The messaging should be tailored, as most attendees will have a common purpose or profession. One-off webinars don't have to be excessively long to be effective. Consider having multiple thirty-minute live sessions that people can attend on the same topic at a time that works best for them. Consider also utilizing two-minute PSA-like clips on social media platforms to help solidify and distribute your message. Longer town hall or panel-style sessions can dive deeper into the issues for those interested after attending a shorter webinar or seeing a social media clip.

Have participants register for each event so that you can follow up with them about future events, actions they can take, and other advocacy messaging. Give every registrant the option to sign up for your organization's newsletter or other preferred online connection platform. Additionally, organizers should allow participants an opportunity to provide feedback and express an interest in further involvement via short online surveys. One efficient way to do this is with a digital survey that gathers contact information and asks three to five questions relevant to the presentation. Having a QR code for the form or survey and a shortened link is effective in both in-person and virtual settings.

Ecosystem representatives from every participating organization should be included at every meeting, and complete records of the discussion should be kept. Cross-communication from the ecosystem team to all participating organizations is essential for transparency and buy-in. Whether the ecosystem initiative is a new aspect of an existing library organization or a stand-alone team bringing together independent library organizations, this persistent and consistent two-way communication will be critical to every success.

Communication with Advocacy Allies

Just as we do well to work collaboratively across library professions and types, we should remember to expand our ecosystem to include other similarly aligned groups. Teachers' unions can be strong allies for school library-related causes, and library organization members are often union members who can bridge that communication pathway and facilitate cooperation.

Advocacy allies for intellectual freedom abound in today's world. LGBT groups, the American Civil Liberties Union, and Black Lives Matter have joined the collective voices against censorship in school libraries in recent years. The attacks on intellectual freedom in American schools and libraries are now multipronged, strategic, and intensely focused. Often, a few agitators manipulate the current processes, such as public comment platforms at board meetings, to chip away at intellectual freedom. These attacks are strategic and persistent; therefore, our efforts must also be strategic and tenacious.

When building support across the ecosystem, try to use all forms of digital communication that are available to maximize your reach. This means discussion lists, newsletters, various social media platforms, and when possible, texts. It often works well to have one person in charge of distributing information to social media, so long as everyone creating content knows who that person is and how to get content to them. It also works well to designate a team to develop the content to ensure a consistent style and quality before things are posted too quickly.

Deeper communication is needed once you have gotten attention for your cause through social media posts, newsletters, news articles, and infographics. Communication from the organization should employ common language, talking points, agenda items, and action steps to share with potential advocates. The advocacy team should have "60-second advocacy" steps that people can take immediately. "One-click" communication tools are powerful platforms that should not be overlooked.

Make advocacy a key topic at in-person events. State library associations typically carry out two functions. They are professional organizations that support networking, collaboration, and learning, and they are often the only statewide group designed to specifically address library-related causes. A strong state library association can do both of these things effectively and in tandem. The Ecosystem Continuum offers new tools to support any group working to build awareness of positive library impacts to increase support for those libraries.

Annual state library associations' conferences can effectively achieve both goals when planned with that dual purpose in mind. Advocacy should be woven into every conference and available to all participants, not just those attending committee meetings. When presenting your advocacy agenda at conferences, give people a way to take action then and there. One way to do this is by having everyone e-mail a thank-you note to supportive legislators. Some other forms of media include signs, slides, and business cards with QR codes to send a form letter to a legislator, having a postcard or petition on hand, or a social media message that can be easily amplified and shared. The leadership should enlist new volunteers and give them a role or duty when they express interest.

Public-Facing Communications

Communicating our objectives and needs to the public is crucial to advocacy work. We must be eloquent and outspoken in defense of libraries' values, namely our First Amendment rights of intellectual freedom and free speech. Newspaper showcases and editorials that highlight the unified stance librarians take for intellectual freedom—and why we fight so hard for it—can help people understand the value of supporting libraries, even if they don't see themselves as library users.

Even if these blanket communication efforts don't bring in new outspoken advocates, the sway of public opinion plays an important role when policy and government decisions are being made. Policymakers at all levels constantly listen for indications of what their communities prioritize.

Additionally, public-facing accounts of advocacy efforts and plans inform readers that the librarians are standing firm and that Mr. and Ms. Community Member will not be alone when they speak out in favor of libraries and intellectual freedom.

Legislative-Facing Communications

Any strong advocacy organization will have a list of key contacts, such as supportive legislators on relevant legislative committees, local leaders who profess a love for libraries, and at least one sympathetic person on the governor's staff.

Furthermore, the state library association should have regular, positive communication with the secretary of state or other relevant state officials as often as possible. Historically, libraries have traditionally been an uncomplicated area of responsibility, an easy win—but these days, in the current political environment, we know that relationship is much more fraught. Given this, collaborations and public displays of mutual respect and support can be beneficial to both the secretary of state's office and the library community.

Invite key contacts, such as the secretary of state, local House and Senate representatives, school board members, or other influential community members to your library for an in-person meeting and library tour. These meetings highlight the fantastic work a library can do and the rectifiable deficits in library staffing, funding, and support.

These meetings can also combat the images being put forward by the agitators and book-banners and can replace negativity with enthusiasm for public spaces that support strong communities. Anyone in the library ecosystem can give a tour of the library. It does not have to be an assigned advocacy leader, and it may be a great way for librarians who want to contribute but don't want to get directly involved in policy issues.

Keep your communications with legislators concise and persistent. Printed items are discouraged, but if used, they should be no more than one page, with small bites of critical information and a way for readers to learn more. Legislators tend to prefer electronic communication and strategic, productive in-person or virtual meetings. E-mails should be well-written and stripped of their non-essential content. Flowery language will get you nowhere, but a concise ask and good grammar will open many doors. Make sure there is a straightforward way for the recipient to contact a knowledgeable advocate or library representative with any questions.

Additionally, it is essential to craft the message in a way that helps the legislator see why supporting libraries strengthens communities and their own overall standing within their community.

Sample Form Letter for Contacting Representatives

Dear Representative:

I write to you today on behalf of the Washington Library Association in support of *Senate Bill 5102*. This bill would remove the language "as deemed necessary" from the current law pertaining to school library programs in Washington. Doing so will ensure that every student has access to a school library program overseen by a certified teacher-librarian, as already provided for in the prototypical funding model.

Access to certified teacher-librarians positively correlates to improved student outcomes in multiple measures, including test scores and graduation rates. Additionally, certified teacher-librarians are the most qualified educators to teach digital citizenship, a component of Basic Education in our state.

Washington state has an inequitable distribution of school library programs despite funding being designated explicitly for such programs. This bill will ensure that funding for school library programs is being used appropriately and that qualified teacher-librarians oversee the school libraries across our state.

Thank you for considering SB 5102 / HB 1609 as you begin the 2023 legislative session.

Respectfully,
Your Constituent

Always remember to say "Thank you." Simple expressions of gratitude at every step will encourage the continuity of relationships and increase the chances of successful advocacy year after year, even as leadership and volunteers change. Acknowledge any legislator who has contributed to securing the initiative's goals, so that they feel noticed and appreciated. These "warm and fuzzy" gestures will encourage future relationships with and support from those legislators.

Position Statements as an Advocacy Tool

Advocacy efforts must focus on both in-network and broader communication efforts. For example, placing a position statement on a particular issue on the library organization's website is useful, but it is not advocacy. For it to become advocacy, that position statement must be actively shared with relevant stakeholders, policymakers, the press, and the larger community. The timely release of position statements increases their effectiveness. Therefore, the organization should have a communication policy with a decision tree that can be implemented as needed.

A position statement that represents an organization must be created with all stakeholders in mind and crafted by many hands. It should be approved by the leadership of the groups involved before being distributed. Modern technology, such as living documents like Google Docs, makes this easier than ever before. Multiple contributors can create, edit, and provide feedback in real time, creating a statement that is well-crafted and inclusive of varying viewpoints. Once the position statement exists, it must be approved by the organization's governing bodies. A vote by the executive committee may be sufficient, or your state organization may want its advocacy committee to approve the statement. Ideally, these groups will have at least a few representatives participating in the original drafting of the letter. This approval process is where having a decision tree becomes essential. That process will look very organization-specific and will vary widely depending on the organization's leadership and structure.

Second only to the message itself in importance is its timeliness. In today's world of up-to-the-minute news and social media buzz, responding to both positive and negative press must occur within days, sometimes even hours, before the message becomes either a runaway train or a forgotten blip. The person responsible for sending out press releases, editorials, and social media responses should have a clear chain of action and process for approval, in addition to a list of media contacts and advocates who can speak to the topic at hand. There are many communication models and decision flow charts to choose from. Your state organization must decide which one will allow the group to speak effectively and efficiently with a collective voice.

Facets of Communication Success

Effective communication must be multidirectional, concise, and consistent. Websites, media contacts, e-mail lists, virtual meetings, collaborative documents, phone calls, position statements, congressional testimony, and face-to-face discussions are all necessary for effective communication. However, what matters more than *how* your messages are delivered are the relationships you foster both within and outside the walls of your organization. An effective use of communication tools and strategies lays the track, but the relationships drive the train.

COLLABORATION BUILDS SUCCESS

Sara Kelly Johns

etworking matters. Librarians appreciate working with other librarians, confronting the profession's challenges together, and enjoying the camaraderie involved in making a difference. We learn from our library colleagues by sharing our questions and offering solutions. We coordinate and collaborate with other libraries in our communities to meet the needs of the people we serve. However, when core values are challenged or an initiative needs broader support, cooperation and coordination must move up on the collaboration continuum to become true collaboration.[1] A formal and dedicated ecosystem will guide groups that want to work together with well-designed and ready-to-go directions for action.

Strength with Stakeholders

The inclusivity of this ecosystem model for collaborative coalitions is one of its key strengths. It recognizes the vital role that various stakeholders play in supporting libraries. These stakeholders include, but are not limited to:

- Different types of libraries (public, academic, school, special, etc.)
- Library professional organizations or associations
- Library workers and volunteers

- Trustees, Friends groups, and foundations that support libraries
- Library vendors and service providers
- Literacy and educational organizations
- Community groups
- Employee unions
- Authors and publishers

A library ecosystem with members from among these groups is powerful. The core values shared by all libraries unite us when it becomes time to support and defend libraries. Identifying potential partners and inviting them to be part of an ecosystem team benefits all members and their communities. Including the groups listed above as part of an ecosystem team does not just provide moral support; the team is speaking with *One Voice*—and that voice is louder.

Starting the Collaborative Journey

It is often a personal connection that leads library associations or librarians from constituent groups to start working collaboratively. It takes as few as two people facing an issue, such as pending legislation or censorship attempts, to make a connection. The path to success is more certain when the initial leaders identify shared goals and potential agendas before reaching out to other like-minded people. Recruiting a more extensive group whose members are willing to invest time outside their demanding jobs is challenging for collaborative efforts. However, when action steps are provided, the process becomes simpler for front-end work.

Developing an Agenda

The first task for an ecosystem initiative is to build an agenda for action.

Legislative advocacy is directed towards the legislative process, with a goal of inspiring elected officials to formally support libraries in general or on a specific issue or piece of legislation (funding, censorship, staff certification, etc.).

Advocacy for public awareness works to increase communities' understanding of how libraries support them, why they are essential to the broader community, and how residents' support helps libraries remain vibrant.

The content of the action agenda may be the same in each path, but the methods and audiences differ. In the legislative effort, you communicate with elected officials who want to please their constituents. In raising public awareness, you guide potential voters who will elect those legislators but who may not be as aware of significant issues. Explaining how libraries work and why they matter is how you create impact in this arena. Within each path, advocates must focus on specific goals to be most effective. It is tempting to tackle all the issues in each category, but focusing on your most significant issue and putting your energy there will be more productive.

The "Ecosystem Agenda Building Templates" (appendix A), which are part of the "Implementation Guide for Strong Library Ecosystems," outline steps that organizations' leadership can follow to create momentum:

1. Focus on the issues in front of you.
2. Develop a potential list of partners from all library types and organizations that are interested in libraries' success.
3. Gather input from all organizations.
4. Consolidate the input.
5. Develop a shared agenda.
6. Send the agenda to all partners for review.
7. Share the results, conclusions, and plans with stakeholders from all partners.
8. Build on the strengths and connections of your collaborative groups for action.[2]

Shared Leadership

With the development of a prospective agenda, taking the time for a conscious look at shared leadership can facilitate working together for the same goal. Defining shared leadership to include everyone focused on an issue is crucial for problem-solving and decision-making. The University of Kansas's "Community Tool Box" explores the usefulness of collaborative leadership and how to practice it effectively, and it is worth perusing.[3]

The experts David Chrislip and Carl Larson propose in the "Community Tool Box" that "if you bring the appropriate people together in constructive ways with good information, they will create authentic visions and strategies for addressing the shared concerns of the organization or community."

The Ecosystem Toolkit delineates specific traits that characterize collaborative leadership. Among the most important of these traits are:

- *Collaborative problem-solving and decision-making.* It is not the leader's job to decide what to do and then tell the group. Instead, the group considers the problem, decides what to do, and counts on the leader to help them focus their effort.
- *Open process.* In collaborative leadership, the leader doesn't merely start with personal goals and guide the group accordingly. Instead, the decision-making process involves active participation from all members, and lacks a predetermined end point at the start. The outcome is a product of the collective effort of all participants—this is genuine collaboration.
- *Leading the process, not the group.* Collaborative leadership aims to help the collaborative process work rather than to lead the people involved toward a particular decision or direction.

Aligning Vocabulary

As leaders and stakeholders work together to reach the same goals, they often discover that they don't have the same vocabulary for essential terms. Groups must consider the collective meaning of such questions as "What is intellectual freedom?" "How does advocacy work?" "How do you define information literacy?" When language is clear and unifying, the collective voice becomes more robust.

Assessing Your Strengths

A burgeoning coalition can use a self-assessment tool to develop a more focused direction. The "One Voice: A Continuum for Stronger Library Ecosystems" collaboration rubric, available in Chapter 3 and the online Ecosystem Toolkit, can help you determine your collaboration status.[4]

Consider the following question: Is your group beginning, is it already evolving, or is the group highly effective? It is common for groups to be *highly effective* in some areas and *beginning* in others. Start where you are.

The "One Voice: A Continuum for Stronger Library Ecosystems" Collaboration Rubric

Sharing between Organizations

Beginning: Initial representatives share priorities with the group to begin building a collaborative agenda.

Evolving: Representatives work together to identify shared priorities and build a collaborative agenda.

Highly Effective: Representatives maintain a current advocacy and legislative agenda that reflects shared priorities.

Collaborative Agenda and Priorities

Beginning: Initial representatives compile the annual ecosystem agenda from the priorities of each participating organization.

Evolving: Representatives hone an agenda from lists of priorities that forward the agreed mutual goals of the ecosystem.

Highly Effective: Representatives collaborate to build and maintain a current advocacy and legislative agenda that reflects shared priorities.

Events and Resources

Beginning: Representatives from participating organizations attend and participate in other organizations' events.

Evolving: Partner organizations consider participating in the planning and production of each other's events.

Highly Effective: Participating organizations are represented in the planning and production of each other's events, or they co-host events.

Advocacy and Legislative

Beginning: Initial representatives share advocacy and legislative agenda ideas, needs, and priorities with the group.

Evolving: Representatives support collaborative goals by sharing new advocacy and legislative issues and priorities.

Highly Effective: Representatives collaborate to build and maintain a current advocacy and legislative agenda that reflects shared priorities.

Collaboration in Action: Legislative Success in New Jersey

When the New Jersey Association of School Librarians (NJASL) began its quest to get school librarians formally included and specifically named in their state's education standards, they had an existing library ecosystem that included the New Jersey Library Association (NJLA). NJLA and NJASL together conducted a joint survey to determine the status of school libraries and librarians in New Jersey. Measured in this report were school librarian needs; the results were alarming to both groups and indicated an immediate need for action to increase the impact of school librarians on the lives of the state's students.[5]

Working together, NJLA and NJASL developed an easy-to-read chart showing the differences and similarities between public librarians and school librarians. The chart became a strong advocacy tool with legislators, their staff, and community groups, while recruiting them as partners in legislative advocacy efforts. Members of ALA's Ecosystem Subcommittee later added a column to the chart that included the roles of academic librarians, expanding its usefulness for meaningful collaboration. (See appendix C, "A Comparison of Public, School, and Academic Libraries: Vital to Our Communities.")

Though other state library associations (Illinois and Delaware) have been successful at including media literacy taught by school librarians (or library media specialists) in their state education standards, NJASL found that "information literacy" was a term more easily understood and supported, so that is the term they used in their efforts. While led by NJASL, effective collaboration was made easier by the development of templates for messages sent to legislators from their constituents, as well as workshops and infographics, in a campaign that mobilized activism by a collaborative library ecosystem. The successful effort to get a bill (S. 588) through the state legislature and signed by the governor relied on support from educational and community supporters—and persistence.

The NJASL credits the fact that information literacy standards have now become a required part of instruction in New Jersey's K-12 school curriculums to the efforts of the strong library ecosystem team comprised of NJASL, NJLA, the New Jersey Education Association, and various community and legislative supporters. See chapter 17 for the rest of the story!

Collaboration in Action: Virginia Librarians Protect Intellectual Freedom

Together, the Virginia Library Association (VLA) and the Virginia Association of School Librarians (VAASL) collaborated in responding to political efforts in Virginia aimed at censoring instructional materials and school library collections. VLA supports Virginia's public librarians, while VAASL's members are school librarians. VLA's executive director, Lisa Varga, and the VAASL presidents had already communicated about issues of common interest, and personal connections were already present. However, working effectively together for advocacy requires even more intense communication between associations.

In 2013, Virginia parent Laura Murphy petitioned the Fairfax County School Board to require that Toni Morrison's book *Beloved* be removed from the Advanced Placement (AP) English curriculum.[6] She then tried to get the school board and the Virginia Department of Education to require parental consent for any sexually explicit material in curriculum or library resources. Murphy led a campaign to get legislation passed that would censor school materials. It passed, but then-Governor McAuliffe vetoed the bill.

Initially, not all members of VLA were prepared to support the school librarians on censorship issues. Although some VLA members observed that the restrictive legislation specifically targeted instructional materials, and pointed out that VLA members are not school librarians, thus distancing themselves from the issue, the VLA executive committee took a different stance. They recognized the bill as an attack on intellectual freedom, a core value for VLA, and then committed to utilizing the association's full influence to prevent such legislation. This position received support from VLA's members. VLA felt and acted on the belief that an attack on one library type is an attack on intellectual freedom in all libraries. They also noted that it is often less complicated for the least vulnerable—in this case, VLA—to speak up.[7]

The proposed legislation was vetoed by the governor in 2016 and 2017, and the situation seemed stable. But in 2021, the same parent used an event in the gubernatorial race to bring censorship efforts to the table again. When Glenn Youngkin was elected governor, part of his Day One Game Plan was to sign legislation that required parents to sign permission slips to give their children the right to sign out "sexually explicit" books. This event led VLA and VAASL to collaborate more closely. Introducing herself as "I am Lisa Varga and I am a taxpayer, don't waste my tax money," Varga presented an invoice for $400,000 to the Virginia Beach School Board for the extra work required of school librarians due to challenges. She later gave the school board an additional invoice for nearly $7,000,000 on September 27, 2022 (figure 6.1). This invoice covered the time required by herself as VLA executive director and by school librarians to process an excessive number of book challenges.[8]

Librarians in Virginia used other collaborative tactics as well. An August 24, 2023, *Library Journal* article reported: "Another effort at VLA involves the creation of 'book résumés' by volunteers. These documents show the ratings, the reviews, the awards, the articles written about it so that our members can have a document to be able to pass on to their trustees and save them the time, Varga said."[9] This idea of being prepared with résumés ready for a challenge has since become an initiative of United Against Book Bans as well.[10]

Another attack on the right to read came with an unsuccessful attempt to keep Barnes & Noble from selling books that some considered

FIGURE 6.1 | **Invoice 000002 to Virginia Beach School Board for approximately $7,000,000**

	INVOICE 000002
Taxpayers	Date: September 27, 2022
Virginia Beach, Va 23456	
Bill To:	
Victoria Manning	
Virginia Beach School Board	
Member at Large	

DESCRIPTION	AMOUNT
16 reconderatins requests x 40 hours per x $1500 hourly wages combined	$ 960,000.00
100 books "found" and intended for reconsideration by petiioner	$ 6,000,000.00

Source: Lisa Varga, Virginia Library Association

sexually explicit.[11] There are more attacks on public libraries. *One Voice*, a *loud* voice, is needed as they deal with adversarial community members. Librarians speak up for students, parents, teachers, administrators, school boards, boards of trustees, taxpayers, local and state legislators, and like-minded organizations.

Making a Difference Together

Collaboration takes a strong commitment to both a shared agenda and action for advocacy, but the time and energy are worth it when your goal is reached.

As the poet Amanda Gorman writes in *Something, Someday*, library ecosystem collaboration can have results that matter:

> Suddenly, there's something
> You're sure is right.
> Something you know
> You helped fix.
> Something small that changed—
> Something big.
>
> Something that worked.
> Something that makes you feel
> Hopeful, happy and loved.
>
> Something that is not a dream
> But the day you live in.
> —*Amanda Gorman*[12]

NOTES

1. Robert Grover, Collaboration, "Proceedings of the American Association of School Librarians Meeting in the Middle Symposium," American Library Association, 1996.
2. American Library Association, "Welcome to the Implementation Guide for Strong Library Ecosystems," www.ala.org/sites/default/files/advocacy/content/stateandlocal/Ecosystem/Ecosystem%20Implementation%20Guide.pdf.
3. University of Kansas, Center for Community Health and Development, "Community Tool Box," https://ctb.ku.edu/en/table-of-contents/leadership/leadership-ideas/collaborative-leadership/main.
4. American Library Association, "One Voice: A Continuum for Stronger Library Ecosystems," www.ala.org/sites/default/files/advocacy/content/Library%20Ecosystem%20Continuum%20Updated.pdf.
5. Maureen Donohue and James Keehbler, *School Library Programs in New Jersey: Building Blocks for Realizing Student Potential with ESSA Legislation Opportunities* (NJASL and NJLA, April 2016), https://njasl.org/resources/Documents/2016ESSAandNJSchoolLibraryPrograms.pdf.

6. T. Rees Shapiro, "Fairfax County Parent Wants 'Beloved' Banned from School System," *Washington Post*, February 2, 2013, www.washingtonpost .com/local/education/fairfax-county-parent-wants-beloved-banned-from -school-system/2013/02/07/99521330-6bd1-11e2-ada0-5ca5fa7ebe79_story .html.

7. Lisa Varga, personal e-mails to Sara Kelly Johns, September 11–25, 2023.

8. Lisa Varga, personal e-mail to Sara Kelly Johns, December 4, 2023.

9. Matt Ennis, "Advocating for the Right to Read: Digipalooza 2023," *Library Journal*, August 23, 2023, www.libraryjournal.com/story/advocating-for -the-right-to-read-digipalooza-2023.

10. Unite Against Book Bans, https://uniteagainstbookbans.org

11. Amanda Haulpuch, "Virginia Judge Dismisses Case That Sought to Limit Book Sales," *New York Times*, August 31, 2022, www.nytimes.com/2022/ 08/31/us/virginia-obscenity-book-ban.html.

12. Excerpt from Amanda Gorman, *Something, Someday* (New York: Viking, Penguin Random House, 2023). Text copyright © 2023 by Amanda Gorman. Used by permission of Viking Children's Books, an imprint of Penguin Young Readers Group, a division of Penguin Random House LLC. All rights reserved.

7

SUSTAINING YOUR ADVOCACY ECOSYSTEM

Dorcas Hand

S o, you've built an ecosystem team. It's taken several months, maybe more. And you've accomplished a goal or two. You've involved a few library organizations and possibly even some library supporter organizations. But you may have managed all that without any formal organization. How will you ensure that this collaborative effort that has borne such useful fruit will continue?

Let's remember how your ecosystem began: a few *leaders* stepped up to find better ways to *communicate* and *collaborate* around advocacy topics across library types and library organizations. Those first leaders were visionaries as they reached out beyond their own organizational silos to open conversations and build collaborative agendas and messaging. The ecosystem leadership team must now facilitate *sustainability* by establishing a pipeline of new leader representatives to represent the same organizations over time, and perhaps to invite in more voices. Sustainability requires ecosystem members to consider how best to ensure that every participating organization remains an enthusiastic member that wants to continue due to their successful interactions. Enthusiastic organizational partners are much more likely to establish an internal system for sending a representative to ecosystem meetings going forward. Sustainability means not only establishing an internal system for bringing new faces to participate in the ecosystem; it also includes encouraging partner organizations to do the same. It may also include inviting additional partners to the table to represent related organizations, perhaps library Friends groups or vendor associations.

Reaching out to other silos can even take place within the same organization. Some state library associations are large, with well-established advocacy efforts and systems. But no system is perfect. Ecosystem ideas offer the potential to bring more ideas and increased transparency to the larger organization. This in turn increases confidence across the membership that the top-level leaders are listening to their members' needs and conveying them to the ecosystem team through the voice of the organization's ecosystem representative. Sustainability policies can stimulate the regular examination of systems and procedures and thus keep transparency and inclusivity at the forefront in order to foster members' and leaders' enthusiasm.

Keeping the Feel of Change

The initial leaders were change agents. Sustainability goals can keep that excitement alive. While the ecosystem is at its core an advocacy tool, you would like it to permanently remain a gathering of change agents, representatives who continue to lead efforts to improve the status quo and develop more effective advocacy programs that reflect the changing needs of the library community's ecosystem. Leader representatives who are consistently strong communicators will be able to lead both the ecosystem team and its partner organizations to strong mutual understandings of their needs and goals as the ecosystem develops and hones its own priorities and agendas. And these leader representatives are excellent at building relationships with both other ecosystem representatives and those among their own organizations.

Building Sustainability

Now that we have considered the underlying philosophy of sustainability in this context, let's consider methods. You have a group of partner organizations. These could be libraries of various types, professional library organizations for those types, and related organizations like Friends groups or vendors. Initially, the group will include those leaders who realized the ecosystem initiative's benefits, the change agents who stepped up. But these leaders may not represent all of the other library associations or organizations in your state or local area. How will you invite these other groups that you realize should be included? How might you take account of their needs in your advocacy efforts, even if they choose not to join yet?

In the beginning your ecosystem group may be small, but it could grow as others see its effectiveness. As in any other organization, rules, policies, and procedures need to be developed to ensure appropriate representation, as well as deciding on mission and vision statements, internal leadership, and so on. What does membership entail? How will you define the organizations that will be partners? How will you ensure that representation is fair and equal for all partner groups? How often will this representation change? Will there be term limits for the representatives? How will you bring new faces up to speed on current topics? How will you ensure that there is term overlap so that only some faces change each year to maintain continuity? (Remember that few projects will end in a single year.) Will there be dues to cover the initiative's operating expenses, or will you operate under the umbrella of an existing organization? And throughout all of this organizational focus, how will you keep the structure simple enough that it feels useful rather than onerous?

Sustaining Leadership

If you have only a few groups partnering in the ecosystem effort, everyone will have a seat at the table. Even so, you will likely need a chair to call the meetings. Will this role rotate in some preordained way? Or will you elect a chair from the member representatives to serve for some regular period (one year, or more)? How often will you meet? Consider meeting at least two or three times a year. Then consider the possibility that you will grow enough to perhaps need a management structure. What might this look like? Do you need officers? Will you need standing committees? Remember that your goal is to maintain fair and equal representation over time, so think about the mechanisms that will facilitate your goal.

Your ecosystem team will need to train new leader representatives (aka "succession planning" or "leadership development"), so that there will be a pool of candidates for every office every time one is needed;

you will need to rely on the partner organizations to help. What procedures can you implement to facilitate their pipelines to your team? Current member representatives will work to raise ecosystem awareness throughout their partner organizations, not just in the officers that are currently deciding organizational priorities. These representatives will continuously demonstrate to their organization the benefits of participating in the ecosystem, and especially the greater diversity of perspectives and ideas that comes from ecosystem work.

Sustaining Membership

Vibrant organizations have enthusiastic members. In this case, you will have representatives of partner organizations on the ecosystem team. Each spokesperson will need to thoroughly understand the advocacy needs of the organization they represent, while also bringing to the ecosystem team the knowledge the other members need. That person will need to understand in depth the collaborative compromises under discussion in ecosystem meetings and convey these to the partner organization they represent to facilitate broad understanding and eager buy-in by that partner. Each representative is thus an essential information conduit who is always working in two directions. This need for frequent and constant communication up and down the line demonstrates the need for clear policies that outline the necessary organizational relationships. It's like breathing in the opinions, ideas, and suggestions from the participating organizations, and breathing out to share with them the resulting collaborative agenda.

Navigating Ecosystem Dynamics

For the ecosystem to be most effective, the group of representatives will need a solid working relationship based on clear policies and guidelines that facilitate the development of strong agendas that all the partners can agree on. Realizing that not every partner will have their top priority recognized in the group agenda every year, it will be important to have strong communication and collaboration over time to ensure that all partners are "featured" equally in the long term. It is also important to maintain an ongoing, inclusive account of diverse ideas and needs that have coalesced into a list of ecosystem priorities. The Ecosystem Toolkit and Continuum offer useful resources to advance this goal, like the "Ecosystem Agenda Building Templates" (appendix A) and the "Comparison of Public, School, and Academic Libraries" (appendix C).[1]

Currently, we must look at the kinds of challenges to intellectual freedom that are now confronting school and public libraries. ALA and state groups have begun to work together and with non-library groups to stand in opposition to these censorship efforts—*that* is an ecosystem in action, albeit an informal one. While these anti-censorship efforts may not have been on the initial agenda of the ecosystem, the importance of responding to them with *One Voice* has become incontrovertible.

Building an Advocacy Calendar

One essential tool for the sustainability of any ecosystem team is a rough annual calendar. Given the fact that some advocacy efforts will probably be focused on government funding or other legislative support, awareness of the legislative calendar of your state will be important. When is the state legislature's normal session? Which are the essential committees with whom to build relationships? If you are working on raising public awareness, the calendar may be looser—but that public awareness (aka voters) has the potential to elect sympathetic legislators. Looking a year or two ahead and mapping your goals by the calendar is always a good practice. For a sample annual calendar, see appendix B, "State & Local Year-Round Advocacy Checklist."

At the same time, partner organizations will need to reflect the ecosystem calendar in their own agenda calendars, so that work on partner group priorities is done in time to support ecosystem planning. If the partner organizations' goals have not been finalized when the ecosystem needs them, the ecosystem cannot easily reflect the needs of those partners, which may contribute to a weaker ecosystem message or a sense that not all member organizations are well represented. Every ecosystem member will need to show up ready to work and contribute.

Measure Your Success

At least once a year, your group should gather together to look at the work you've done to evaluate its success. Even better, when you plan a project, include metrics that will measure its success, so that upon completion you can see how successful the project was in measurable ways. How could the project have been more successful? Or why did it not accomplish its goals as well as hoped? What changes to the plan might have changed the outcome? This process of evaluation will include input from the partner organizations: Do they think the ecosystem served them well? From their perspectives, how could the collaboration have been more successful? Evaluation will likely also reflect the input of constituent groups: can the representatives explain the network's successes to their home organization as a win for them in particular, as well as for the ecosystem as a whole? However it is explained, do the participating organizations feel like the ecosystem work was successful? This periodic review is especially important when a project does not reach its goal—that project may need to be modified and tried again. What methods and tools should be adopted for the redo, and which ones should be modified or dropped?

So at the end of your year, look at all the work completed with an eye to evaluation: Was this work useful? How could it have been more effective overall? Keep reports of these evaluations for reference in the future. One of the best ways to ensure a strong future is to always consider where you have been. Report-writing may seem dull, but institutional accounts of projects that were successful and even those that were imperfect offer lessons for next steps. These reports can be shared with participating organizations to make sure that they remain aware of all the work done, as well as the successes achieved.

Dealing with Dissension

No group agrees all the time, or even most of the time. And in an ecosystem, you are reaching beyond your home silo to work with others whose agendas are not completely in sync with yours. What kinds of procedures will you use to manage that? Robert's Rules? Consensus?

Remember that at every step, the representatives will need to go back to their partner organizations to discuss what is happening in the ecosystem. This increased awareness of how related but different groups think is a real bonus, but it needs care and attention to keep moving forward. Use challenging moments in the discussion as ways to improve the agenda or project. If you can collaborate to include these points of difference as positives, the project is more likely to be accepted by the partner groups. And once you reach agreement, you can speak with *One Voice* to every audience.

Forging a Sustainable Path

A library ecosystem already exists informally or potentially in every state and region. But not all of its members or its audiences realize the truth of this or acknowledge their participation (or lack of such) in it. No library exists in a vacuum; every library overlaps in its mission, community, and content with some other library, and probably several. At the same time, no two libraries are exactly the same even if they are the same "type." As a library community, we face quite a bit of pushback from people who think libraries are too expensive, too inclusive, or are unnecessary. A formal ecosystem builds strength in numbers to develop consistent agendas that are easier for the general public to understand and support, even in the face of naysayers and challengers. For this ecosystem to be successful beyond a single project, it must be sustainable over time and across library types, and able to take advantage of existing formal groups of supporters. Take steps to make your ecosystem as strong and sustainable as possible.

NOTE

1. American Library Association, "Ecosystem Agenda Building: Information Gathering: Template for Building a Collaborative Advocacy Agenda," One Voice, www.ala.org/sites/default/files/advocacy/content/stateandlocal/ Ecosystem/Ecosystem%20Agenda%20Building%20Template%20-%20 Information%20Gathering.docx.pdf; American Library Association, "A Comparison of Public, School, and Academic Libraries: Vital to Our Communities," www.ala.org/sites/default/files/advocacy/content/Ecosystem %20Public%2C%20School%20and%20Academic%20Libraries%20Fact% 20Sheet_0.pdf.

PART III

Applying Ecosystem Ideas

ADVOCACY
Leading from Life

Anthony Chow

have worn many different hats and held different roles in my life: as a library patron, a library professional, a father, as the head of library advocacy for an entire state, and as a full professor and director of the largest MLIS program in the nation. All of these roles have informed this essay. Libraries have always been a part of my ecosystem—from some of my earliest memories as a child to today—as I write these words.

My Life in Libraries

I am the second son of Chinese immigrants, and my parents' dedication to their restaurant business left my brother and me with ample time to spend at the public library. Those walls became a gateway to a world of knowledge, supporting us through school projects and academic pursuits.

As I became a husband and father, libraries evolved from a scholarly foundation to a personal partner in raising our children. Storytimes, borrowed books, and summer reading programs enriched our family experiences. The library's role in our lives, guiding our children through endless possibilities, became an integral part of our family narrative.

Entering academia, I leveraged academic libraries for student resources and literature reviews, acknowledging their pivotal role in my scholarly productivity. This appreciation fueled my involvement in the advocacy and legislative committee of the North Carolina Library Association (NCLA) in 2006. The rise of the internet and digital technology posed challenges to the perceived relevance of libraries and compelled me to support an institution that is integral to my life.

Over the past seventeen years, my advocacy journey has taken me across the country, advocating for libraries at various levels, including a memorable day spent with the ALA president on Capitol Hill. This chapter encapsulates the experiences and insights I've gained through these advocacy endeavors, emphasizing the enduring importance of libraries in shaping individual and community narratives.

Let's begin.

Advocacy Nuts and Bolts: Theory, Context, and Action

The "magic" ingredient of effective advocacy is *you*. Your personal conviction as a library advocate, your values and stories, and all the nuts-and-bolts work you do in the background are all critical and essential. A person's ability to truly make a difference and advocate effectively often comes down to that person's relationship with the person being advocated to.

The Public Library Association defines advocacy as: "The actions individuals or organizations undertake to influence decision-making at the local, regional, state, national, and international level that help create a desired funding or policy change in support of public libraries."[1]

The *Merriam-Webster Dictionary* defines advocacy as "the act or process of supporting a cause or proposal: the act or process of advocating for something."[2]

The American Association of School Librarians provides us with a library-oriented definition of advocacy: an "ongoing process of building partnerships so that others will act for and with you, turning passive support into educated action for the library program. It begins with a vision and a plan for the library program that is then matched to the agenda and priorities of stakeholders."[3]

ALA's Ecosystem Initiative takes a systems approach to library advocacy and notes that we are all part of one macro-level ecosystem. More specifically, "a library ecosystem is the *interconnected* network of all types of libraries, library workers, volunteers, and associations that provide and facilitate library services for community members—families; K-12 learners; college and university communities; local, state and federal legislatures and government offices; businesses; nonprofits; and other organizations with specific information needs."[4] So, looking at these four definitions, our working definition of advocacy is simply: "Our/your *action* to *influence* decision-making and to *support* a cause/proposal."

The ALA's definition focuses on interconnectedness and a library ecosystem that unites all libraries, their workers, the patrons who use those libraries, and other sectors of society that sometimes depend on libraries. The act of advocacy occurs at all levels—individual, local, state, and national—and involves turning a lack of support into "educated action" in support of libraries.

Alan Inouye states that libraries are considered a golden policy item on Capitol Hill and that there are no significant critics of the innate value of libraries. It is not that members of Congress are not supportive of libraries, but rather a question of where libraries fit in to their current funding priorities. Alan states:

> Libraries and the association both have a golden reputation in DC and in DC policy circles. It's very rare to find someone who is really against us, or has a bad feeling or anything like that, and usually it's a very positive one, and that many groups want to collaborate with us or to partner with us. Whether they're other advocacy groups, or even members of Congress in their offices, they actually reach out to us.[5]

Megan Cusick, the former assistant director of state advocacy in ALA's Public Policy and Advocacy Office, says a similar warmth exists on the local levels as well, and polling consistently finds strong support for libraries:

> Overall libraries have a tremendous amount of support in their local communities, and even at the State level. Polling shows that the vast majority, in the realm of ninety percent of voters, believe that libraries, both school and public, are important to their communities. So that is really an overwhelmingly favorable view. They also have similar opinions about library staff.[6]

A Review of the Literature

The "Advocacy Strategy Framework" (figure 8.1) provides a visual representation of the strategies needed to create change at three levels—awareness, will, and action—across three levels of audiences—the public, influencers, and decision-makers. Overall, they suggest that an advocacy strategy should embrace twenty-two activities.

FIGURE 8.1 | The Advocacy Strategy Framework: A tool for articulating an advocacy theory of change

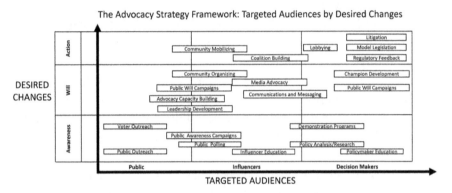

The Advocacy Strategy Framework: Targeted Audiences by Desired Changes

Source: Re-created from J. Coffman and T. Beer, "The Advocacy Strategy Framework," Center for Evaluation Innovation, 2015; the framework was first cited by J. Coffman in *Foundations and Public Policy Grantmaking* (2008).

In "Advocacy Is All of Us: Recommendations to Enhance the Medical Library Association's Advocacy Initiatives," JJ Pionke et al. share their findings from interviews with ten experts and survey responses from 340 participants from the field with regard to advocacy recommendations.[7]

The interviews found three primary themes for effective advocacy:

1. Relationship-building
2. Showcasing value
3. Strengthening the interpersonal advocacy skills of librarians

The surveys found that librarians have two primary advocacy gaps:

1. Articulating the value of their library
2. Advocating for needed resources

In her article "How to Articulate Your Library's Impact and Get What You Need," Lisa Peet found that the ability to effectively articulate libraries' impact involves *data* and a *narrative* that is well-targeted and well-crafted.[8] One must also convey a knowledge of your audience and their priorities. More specifically, Peet suggests ten things to do. In summary, you should:

1. Know your audience—do your homework about what they care most about, identify tangible ways they can help, and build short and long-term relationships.
2. Perfect the pitch—clearly identify and convey both libraries' needs and achievements.
3. Keep advocacy a priority—outline who you want to talk with and when (and also how).
4. Learn the issues; they are a way in—given the fact that legislators already have an affinity for libraries, try to find ways in which libraries align with the legislators' own priorities.
5. Go big (or else go home)—library usage and funding are increasing at many levels, and so it is important to swing for the fences in terms of what you need to do the job, and not be too conservative in what you're asking for.
6. Evaluate outcomes—be very clear on what the short- and long-term outcomes of your library's project, program, or impact will be, identify ways to measure the outcomes, and then build a system to do just that.
7. Emphasize the return on investment (ROI)—look for ways to measure and articulate both the costs of the library and the return realized by patrons and the community at large; the ROI almost always is positive, and libraries return much more than the cost of their resources, programs, and projects.
8. Understand the value of marketing—there is also a clear ROI of the costs of library marketing and the return on that marketing in terms of users, reading, visitation, and programs.

9. Include narratives and numbers—have at your fingertips the typical circulation and usage stats, but also have personal stories about how real people are using your library and the impact on them; remember, decision-makers are just like you and I, and everyone likes a feel-good story.

10. Compromise—try and avoid the "my way or the highway" approach, where not getting what you want is deemed a failure or lacking in success; always be grateful for any funding for libraries, no matter how large or small it is.

In "Advocacy 101 for Academic Librarians: Tips to Help Your Institution Prosper," Terry Kirchner emphasizes that advocacy is not really about focusing on one decision-maker, but rather is "the act of pleading for or supporting a change in an *existing system* which will produce results that are permanent and will benefit future users of the system."[9] Kirchner includes Elizabeth Bingham's 13 Principles of Advocacy:

1. Know your case; document facts.
2. Know the opposing case and its arguments and develop strategies (e.g., understand the rationale for the lack of support and develop data-driven arguments against them).
3. Operate from a sound base of support.
4. Know your resources and allies.
5. Intervene high enough to get the job done (e.g., advocate at the right level of decision-making to make a difference).
6. Take a positive approach.
7. Demonstrate to the system how it is interfering with or defeating its own goal (e.g., if you want to improve the quality of life for the community, you need to increase rather than decrease library funding and services).
8. Use overt power only after using the first seven principles.
9. When in a power contest, don't pussyfoot around.
10. Use an advocacy effort to strengthen your group.
11. Always be aware of vulnerability.
12. Assess risks realistically; identify them; and weigh them against gains.
13. Don't play the devil's advocate.[10]

Although Bingham identified these principles in 1995, they all still apply today. There are two more principles we should add now:

- Use technology, especially social media.
- Make it personal—relationships are everything.

Kirchner also succinctly states why advocacy is important for all LIS professionals: "Although libraries and librarians are often not in the business of doing business, we should look to see what core practices could help ensure that libraries stay in business."[11]

Jamie LaRue is renowned for his work with the Douglas County Libraries, and specifically for "taking one of the worst library systems in Colorado" and turning it into one of the strongest systems in the nation.[12] His secret to success? The power of the narrative and storytelling. LaRue posits that the best stories have six elements: (1) a real person, (2) a real problem, (3) a library intervention, (4) a happy ending, (5) a single fact, and (6) a tagline. More specifically, in collaboration with the OCLC and ALA, the four key messages are:

- Libraries transform lives.
- Libraries transform communities.
- Librarians are passionate advocates for lifelong learning.
- Libraries are a smart investment.[13]

LaRue also notes that, based on ALA's Advocacy Bootcamps, the best advocates are often not the librarian but rather a "community member who can offer unbiased support."[14]

The Psychology of Decision-Making

Decision-making is either goal-directed or habitual, according to Raab and Hartley.[15] Research suggests that younger people are more goal-directed, while older people (which defines most decision-makers) rely more on habits or patterns of behavior based on years of experience.[16] In order to influence a decision-maker and help them see why voting for your cause is the best way to go, you have to address both these factors:

you have to show them how your issue or cause is aligned with their goal-directed behavior; and, if needed, you have to "disrupt" their habitual or lifelong perception of libraries, and do so within the context of their other pressing and important social spending priorities.

Dietrich highlights the importance of four factors that affect a person's decision-making: (1) past experience, (2) age and individual differences, (3) belief in personal relevance, and (4) escalation of commitment.[17]

When they're unfamiliar with a particular topic or issue, decision-makers tend to fall back on their experience and cognitive biases (stereotypes or mental schemas), which leads them to either dismiss something or give it more credence than it deserves, based on their prior knowledge and expectations. In terms of age and individual differences, research has found that older adults prefer fewer options and fall back on their past experiences. This is why getting decision-makers into libraries and showing them the library's impact on the community helps plant a mental picture in their minds they will rely on when it comes to making future decisions. As far as personal relevance goes, people will be more active or likely to act if they feel their decision or vote matters.

Advocacy Best Practices

Advocacy is an information-seeking exchange, in which a decision-maker or their aide takes the time to talk to you or to read the material you've provided. This means that one of the core principles of information-seeking, Poole's Principle of Least Effort, is in effect: people will expend the least amount of energy to get what they want or meet their goals. This is even more important when you're communicating with leaders who are busy and have a lot of information being provided to them about multiple topics from multiple people.

In short, when doing advocacy, you must deliver memorable material in a short amount of time for busy and tired decision-makers. What is your elevator pitch? What do you want the leader to do and vote for or against? Why? What happens if they don't support or even oppose what you want?

This is why I particularly like Jamie LaRue's focus on the power of the *story* and *tagline*—these provide something that is easy to remember, that likely resonates with a person's emotions, and ends with a quick statement of impact.

From short-term to long-term, here is what I have learned over the years:

1. *Contact information*, and multiple means of communication are essential so that you can share with other people to advocate. Providing contact information makes it much easier for potential advocates to respond to your call to action.

2. *Relationships.* Build relationships with local, county, state, and national leaders by actively participating in their gatherings and community forums. This long-term strategy proves effective when seeking their support. Try to establish connections with office staff, as they often appreciate engaging with LIS advocates. Additionally, consider identifying allies among the legislators' relatives or acquaintances who share a friendly disposition toward the cause—their support can be instrumental in championing your efforts.

3. *Resonance* with decision-makers hinges on aligning your library initiatives with their legislative priorities. Research their focus areas and try to connect library services, resources, and impactful stories to these areas, to ensure alignment amid competing funding choices.

4. *Have clear asks and leave-behinds.* Remember, decision-makers are meeting with their constituents all the time. Make sure you have clear "asks" or things you want them to do. Leave behind material—often both on paper and via an e-mail attachment or link to a website—so they can refer to it when the actual vote looms.

5. *Visitors can be essential.* Decision-makers want to talk to their constituents. But during legislative days making contact with them can be difficult, as there are often not enough advocates to reach out to every office in a limited amount of time. So do the best you can to have actual voters and their constituents at the meeting—every vote counts, and the legislators know this. Also, we have found that K-12 children and constituents who reflect their legislative priorities really resonate with legislators too. Remember, the best advocates are not us but rather our patrons and cus-

tomers. Some of the most effective library advocates have been the children of our library advocates.

6. *Data.* In assessment and evaluation, we refer to data as either inputs (resources), outputs (how you use the resources and results), or outcomes (the impact of your programs, services, and resources). Remember, legislators are not likely to spend a lot of time reading over your material, so you should leave them something they can easily read and understand.

7. *Stories.* To convey the profound impact of libraries to decision-makers, try to have them engage with patrons waiting outside before the library opens. Otherwise, collect a range of stories, and by applying the concepts outlined in this chapter—relevance, impact, outcomes—choose diverse patron narratives. Share these stories in a compelling, personable manner that resonates with the priorities of your decision-maker.

Advocacy Best Practices Checklist

Here is a checklist of nine best practices to keep in mind. Use it to build your core advocacy resources and skills so that you're doing the best you can to inform others about why they should support and fund libraries.

Effective advocacy requires concise, memorable communication. Key practices include:

- *Relationship-building:* Establish contacts with decision-makers, attend events, and arrange tours.
- *Showcasing value:* Highlight inputs, outputs, and outcomes through data and stories.
- *Interpersonal advocacy skills:* Involve everyone in advocacy, fostering a positive relationship with decision-makers.
- *Data:* Demonstrate your knowledge of library trends and their impact on funding decisions.
- *Narrative and stories:* Use personal stories to resonate emotionally with decision-makers.

- *Short and long-term issues:* Prepare material for ongoing advocacy efforts, emphasizing different aspects.
- *Decision-making is goal-directed and/or habitual:* Align your advocacy efforts with decision-makers' goals and disrupt their habitual perceptions.
- *Be diverse:* Use various communication channels for a comprehensive advocacy approach.
- *Build teams:* Form advocacy teams to share the workload and build a community of advocates.

In the end, any activity focused on advocating for libraries is helpful. Alan Inouye, ALA's executive director of public policy and advocacy, says: "[Library advocacy] . . . is just kind of a natural part of the spectrum of library work . . . It's not like a special thing that you know [or] do. . . . It's really just part of your job [and] . . . a professional responsibility."[18]

Rest assured, your passion for the field and the work you do for your patrons and customers is a magic ingredient that will resonate with decision-makers—just work on how you articulate that passion so that the decision-maker will pay attention and hear you. And just in case you were wondering, the practices identified here also apply to advocating for yourself within your own organization as well. That, however, is a story for another time.

NOTES

1. Public Library Association, "Understanding Advocacy," Turning the Page: Supporting Libraries, Strengthening Communities, www.publiclibrary advocacy.org/understanding-advocacy/.
2. *Merriam-Webster Dictionary*, "Advocacy," www.merriam-webster.com/dictionary/advocacy. Emphasis added.
3. American Association of School Librarians, "What Is Advocacy?" www.ala.org/aasl/advocacy/definitions. Emphasis added.
4. American Library Association, "State Ecosystem Initiative," www.ala.org/advocacy/state-ecosystem-initiative.
5. "SJSU iSchool Advocacy Podcast," directed by Anthony Chow, performed by Megan Murray Cusick and Alan S. Inouye, YouTube, 2022, www.youtube.com/watch?v=avWK5B0ilXU.

6. "SJSU iSchool Advocacy Podcast."

7. JJ Pionke, K. Phillips, A. Migdalski, and E. M. Smith, "Advocacy Is All of Us: Recommendations to Enhance the Medical Library Association's Advocacy Initiatives," *Journal of the Medical Library Association* 110, no. 1 (2022): 5–14, https://doi.org/10.5195/jmla.2022.1327.

8. Lisa Peet, "How to Articulate Your Library's Impact and Get What You Need," *Library Journal*, 2020, www.libraryjournal.com/story/Stats-Story -How-to-Articulate-Your-Librarys-Impact-and-Get-What-You-Need.

9. Terry Kirchner, "Advocacy 101 for Academic Librarians: Tips to Help Your Institution Prosper," *College & Research Libraries News* 60, no. 10 (1999): 844–49, https://doi.org/10.5860/crln.60.10.844.

10. Elizabeth E. Bingham, "Library Advocacy," *LLA Bulletin* 58 (Fall 1995): 86, as quoted in Kirchner, "Advocacy 101," 845.

11. Kirchner, "Advocacy 101," 845.

12. James LaRue, "Advocacy and the Power of Narrative: Storytelling as a Fund-raising Tool," *American Libraries*, October 23, 2018, https://americanlibraries magazine.org/2018/10/23/advocacy-bootcamp-power-of-narrative/.

13. LaRue, "Advocacy and Power of Narrative."

14. LaRue, "Advocacy and Power of Narrative."

15. H. A. Raab and C. A. Hartley, "More Than Two Forms of Pavlovian Prediction," *Nature Human Behaviour* 3, no. 3 (2019): 212–13.

16. Cody Kommers, "Why Wisdom Doesn't Work as Well as We Think It Does," *Psychology Today*, February 25, 2019, www.psychologytoday.com/us/blog/ friendly-interest/201902/why-wisdom-doesnt-work-well-we-think-it-does.

17. Cindy Dietrich, "Decision Making: Factors That Influence Decision Making, Heuristics Used, and Decision Outcomes," *Inquiries Journal* 2, no. (2010).

18. "SJSU iSchool Advocacy Podcast."

9

LEVERAGING THE ECOSYSTEM FOR EFFECTIVE LEGISLATIVE ADVOCACY

Eryn Duffee

T he strength of an ecosystem lies in its ability to speak with *One Voice*. If we break down the silos of librarianship—region, library type, roles, target audience, and so on—and create a single, collaborative advocacy agenda, we will be more effective advocates. This cohesion is especially critical when we look at legislative advocacy.

Our message must be *informed, coordinated, concise, and consistent* to be effective. Policymakers are inundated with requests, initiatives, and causes every day. To rise above the din, we must be strategic in communicating our goals. Additionally, we must understand how the legislative process works so that we can effectively move our initiatives through the system and target our work for maximum effect. Then the work of implementation begins.

Build a Legislative Agenda

Your legislative agenda may be based on a critical need for advocacy, as with recent state censorship efforts or decreases in funding. Swift and effective efforts are essential in those instances. However, a sustained advocacy effort will be most effective over time because of the relationships with legislators and standing committees in state government. Having a structure that builds and sustains the advocacy agenda is akin to the steel girders of a high-rise: it is foundational, but not rigid or final. (See appendix A for tools that can help you build an agenda.)

Survey Member Groups

When building a legislative agenda, one starts by learning the priorities of different library types and member groups within the library ecosystem. This is done by surveying individuals in leadership roles on boards and committees. The ecosystem team or organizational leadership then compiles the results to determine what common themes and goals can be unifying factors in advocacy efforts.

The data gathered by this endeavor will also illuminate advocacy objectives that might, on the surface, appear only to affect one library type or region. However, the need could be urgent enough to become a unifying priority. In this instance, having an established culture of mutual support and cohesive advocacy will create a more effective push for priority goals when the time arises. Mutual benefit does not have to be synchronous, but collaboration should be consistent.

Issues That Might Inform Legislative Advocacy Priorities

There are many issues that libraries advocate for. Here are a few common priorities to help you start the conversation.

- Funding
- Staffing
- Broadband and connectivity
- Digital resources
- Access
- Standards

See the "Ecosystem Agenda Building Templates" in appendix A for a detailed template for gathering information on advocacy priorities from all library types in your ecosystem, consolidating that information to see overlaps, and developing collective priorities.

Identify, Prioritize, and Share Goals

Once the various advocacy goals for librarians across the state have been collected, use the cumulative list to identify urgent and shared goals for the ecosystem organization. The Ecosystem Subcommittee of ALA's Committee on Library Advocacy has created agenda-building tools to collect and prioritize the organization's collective advocacy goals and create a year-round advocacy checklist based on those goals. These tools can be found online and in appendixes A and B.

Identifying legislative priorities for the organization should be done each year and well before the upcoming legislative session. Once the leadership has identified priority issues, communicating the collective goals and action steps the membership can take is essential. This can be done through webinars, committee meetings, conference sessions, and newsletters to reach the widest audience possible.

Create an Action Plan

After the collective advocacy agenda has been identified, the year-round advocacy checklist found in appendix B will help maintain the initiative's sustainability by showing advocates what steps to take at each point in the legislative cycle. The checklist can inform meeting agendas and keep the group on task and organized. Effective legislative advocacy *must* occur throughout the year and year after year, with consistent attention to detail. Plan ahead and maintain awareness of when it will be most effective to share your message with legislators—waiting until the last minute dooms the effort. For instance, the time to request sponsorship for a bill is three to four months before the legislative session begins.

Move from Cause to Bill to Law

Let's look at the steps one particular bill related to school libraries took through the Washington State Legislature. While the process will be essentially the same in any state, procedural differences may exist from state to state. Having someone on the advocacy team who understands or has experience with the nuances of your state's legislative pathways is essential.

Decide on the Ask

The School Library Bill, Senate Bill 5727 (and corresponding House Bill 1609) was presented in 2022. It asked to close the loophole that allowed funds already designated for school library programs to be used for other educational expenses within a school district. This loophole siphoned moncy away from school library funding. Moreover, Washington state has no requirements for certified teacher-librarians to staff school library programs, an issue we hoped to rectify.

Be Nimble and Responsive with Your Request

The bill initially asked that school districts with more than 1,000 students have, at the very least, a certified teacher-librarian overseeing the library programs within the district. The Washington Library Association (WLA) wanted additional language that created a school library coordinator position within the Office of the (Washington) Superintendent of Public Instruction (OSPI), but this request was kept out of Bill 5727 to increase the chances that the bill would pass. Plans were made to approach the OSPI directly with this request. With these changes in place, the sponsors submitted the bill to the House and Senate education committees for initial consideration.

Be Prepared to Act Swiftly

In less than two months, the bill had six committee hearings, five committee executive session hearings where it was voted on, and one vote on the floor of the Senate. At each committee hearing, volunteers testified on behalf of school libraries. Student testimonies that shared why teacher-librarians were important to them personally carried significant weight.

Sustain the Effort

Effective change is a marathon. For example, the fight to get funding and certified teacher-librarians in Washington state has been ongoing for at least seven years as of 2023. Within this marathon, there will be sprints; even then, it is helpful to think of them as relays. Sometimes, a core group, or even one person, may need to tackle a particular challenge with zeal and dedication. For the effort to be sustainable, they will need to be able to pass the baton to others when they are unable to dedicate the volunteer hours required to get a bill sponsored, supported, voted on, and passed. Having a core team of dedicated advocates who work well together and support each other is just as essential as any other aspect of organizational work that involves advocacy. This core team represents the members of the library ecosystem.

Create Continuity

Effective communication and documentation will make transitions smoother year after year. For example, unrestricted access to well-kept meeting minutes and agendas will help newcomers understand where things are in the process and how they can contribute in the way that best suits their talents and passions.

Advocates and legislators are in it for the long haul. Key relationships must be built and maintained *before* an intensive push for immediate needs. One builds these relationships through public-facing efforts such as legislative action days at the capital, site visits, public-relations interviews, and photo opportunities.

Build and Leverage Your Brand

Library site visits show legislators what exemplary libraries offer and clarify why legislative and municipal support can help correct any deficits worth noting. Giving legislators a chance to see and be seen in our libraries is a solid investment in relationship-building. As a prime example, certified teacher-librarian Craig Seasholes invited Washington state representative Sharon Tomika Santos, chair of the House Committee on Education, to attend a storytime at his library. This allowed Rep. Santos to see the expanded opportunities libraries bring to education, which inspired her to support school library programs for years to come.

Santos noted three years after this crucial visit, "Craig is my second favorite school librarian, after my own childhood librarian." The relationship-building that Craig did, and the personal connection he formed, were crucial to gaining a key supporter for school libraries in the Washington State Legislature.

The Washington Library Association's Advocacy Committee arranged for Washington Governor Jay Inslee to meet with students and teacher-librarians to discuss the importance of information literacy. The author of this chapter shared a carefully designed presentation on media literacy lessons taught by teacher-librarians with Governor Inslee.

After the short presentation, students shared why they thought information literacy was important and relevant. The students' testimonies and conversations with Governor Inslee and his staff had the most significant impact of the day. Not only were they memorable for the governor and his team, but these student comments also made compelling sound bites that were shared in radio and online news outlets across Washington state.

Be Omnidirectional

The work to support an advocacy movement must be omnidirectional. Grassroots support comes from public awareness. And in turn, public awareness needs to be cultivated daily so your public is ready to be the grassroots you need in a crunch. Advocates already sympathetic to the cause can be constantly encouraged through engagement and persuasive communication. The larger community must see why your cause is significant and beneficial *to them*, and then see how they can help drive its success.

Make Your Case

An advocate's essential task is to convince policymakers that a cause is vital to their constituency, and so supporting the cause benefits the legislators professionally. Politicians regularly respond to a call to action around libraries with quotes like "I love libraries," "My aunt was a librarian," and "I remember my librarian from school." People may have an emotional connection to libraries, but that does not guarantee their support for your advocacy effort.

Once key relationships have been built, the most critical step in pursuing action from legislators is to show political leaders how supporting libraries strengthens their standing with their own constituency. When policymakers *see and hear* that the public supports your cause, they are much more invested in your success because it affects their standing with voters.

Use Available Research and Data

In Washington state, a simple but brilliant infographic showing which counties did not have certified teacher-librarians (figure 9.1), created by LibSlide.org, was an extremely effective tool to show the public and policy makers that there was a problem to be solved.

FIGURE 9.1 | "Where Are There School Librarians?" SLIDE.org

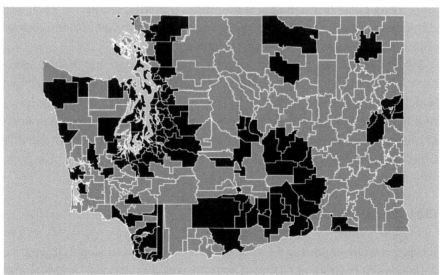

Source: SLIDE.org, "State Profile – SLIDE," https://libslide.org/data-tools/state-profile/?saved =WA&type=stateprofile.

Many conversations with parents and community members showed that people assumed that all schools had libraries and that certified teacher-librarians staffed all school libraries. That is not the case in Washington state. When a three-second glance at an infographic challenges this notion, it has an impact, and grassroots support grows. LibSlide data on every state is available online.

When new supporters can share critical information quickly with their communities, the advocacy efforts are amplified even further. Craig Seasholes would use the LibSlide map of Washington school libraries as his background image when testifying on behalf of the School Library Bill before committee hearings. This "silent but loud" communication effectively showed the need for a more equitable distribution of school library programs to everyone attending the hearing, either in person or virtually.

Stick to the Message

Clear messaging to legislators and the public is essential in all aspects of advocacy work. The group should focus on one or two policy changes they would like to see implemented in a year. When there are too many competing goals or messages at one time, the effectiveness of each one diminishes greatly. This is where the ecosystem mindset and unified coalition-building become crucially important.

For example, a legislative session with twenty library bills on the agenda would be ineffective. By contrast, a legislative agenda with one or two widely supported library bills that don't compete with each other has a much higher chance of becoming law. Once those bills become law, leadership can choose the next legislative priorities. The "Ecosystem Agenda Building Templates" in appendix A will be immensely helpful in this step.

Obtain Legislative Sponsorship

Finding a willing sponsor for your bill is the first official step in legislative action, and it is strategic to find at least one sponsor in both the House and Senate. If you can find multiple sponsors for each bill and possibly bipartisan sponsorship, your bill's chances will be more robust from the start.

Sidestep Lip Service

Legislators will tell you how much they appreciate libraries all day long. However, more in-depth communication will help you see which legislators are truly willing to go to bat for libraries and which ones will stop short of helping you effect change. For example, a legislator whose own wife is a librarian (a point he liked to make often) nevertheless declined to vote Yes on Bill 5727 when it was in his committee. It is a frustrating experience to have a legislator say they will support a bill and then present a bill that doesn't create the change you were looking for. Knowing a legislator's effectiveness and relationships within their committees can also be helpful information.

Make Support Easy for Your Sponsors

Some legislators will want you to provide the bill's language so they can wordsmith it for clarity and the highest chance of success. Other legislators will want to write the bill in their own office and then present it to the advocates in the library organization for approval. Be prepared to work within both scenarios.

Allowing legislative sponsors to utilize this effort for their own public relations is good practice. Invite them to visit school libraries with the media riding along. Sharing the story of the visit with print, online, and social media helps gather support for both the legislator and library advocacy efforts. Once those stories are published, activate your membership to spread them far and wide via newsletters, e-mails, and social media to increase grassroots support for library efforts.

Attend Committee Hearings

A bill's first stop is in committee. Once a bill is sponsored and written, it must be put on a committee's agenda for public hearings. The committee that will consider any bill on its policy merits will hear the bill first, and this is where public testimony from bill supporters—both librarians and community members—is crucial.

Testify at the Hearings

At the hearings, a few coordinated testimonies covering the breadth of information you want the legislators to understand is paramount, and these testimonies should be planned out as a team. Hence, they are impactful and not redundant. There is always the risk of giving too many testimonies, which can decrease support for your cause with legislators if they feel their time is being wasted.

Secondary committees such as finance, rules, or others are less concerned with the merits of the bill and more concerned with its legality and plausibility. Do not overload these committees with testimonials. Instead, have people mark their position on the legislative record, sign petitions, send e-mails, and make phone calls. Library organizations would do well to have members from key legislators' districts contact those legislators, as some legislators will not take comments from anyone outside of their own district.

Make It to the Executive Session

Once a bill has had its public hearing, it needs to get on the agenda for the executive session. This is where the committee will vote on whether or not they pass the bill out of committee. Many bills never make it into the executive session, and so advocacy efforts must continue even after the public hearing to ensure the bill can be voted on. Having someone who can pursue regular communication with a legislator or legislative assistant involved in these decisions can make or break your legislative advocacy. Building those relationships should be ongoing and occur long before a crucial bill is presented.

Be Prepared to Try Again

The School Library Bill in Washington made it through the Senate committee hearings and executive sessions, was passed on the Senate floor, and sent to the House for committee hearings. The bill made it through several House committee sessions and was put on the House Ways and Means Committee's executive season agenda. This was to be the last committee vote before the bill headed to the House floor for what was to be an affirmative vote. The night before the executive committee session, the bill was removed from the agenda, thus preventing it from being voted on and effectively killing the bill. Six months later, the Washington Library Association is still trying to discover who removed the bill from the executive session agenda.

All of this is to say that advocates should be aware that there are many ways for a bill to die. It is entirely possible to gain widespread community and legislative support, make it almost to the finish line, and still not have a law enacted in your favor. However, the process and the publicity garnered among policymakers and the public will help pave the way for future endeavors. In Washington state, legislators and the public alike now have more awareness of the problem, and they see that library advocates are willing and able to fight to obtain school libraries staffed by certified teacher-librarians.

Assist with Implementation

Once a law is passed that affects the libraries in your state, it must be implemented. The library organization can help speed up the adoption of the new policies through a variety of strategic measures. By helping local entities to understand and implement the new regulations, you help ensure that compliance occurs in a productive way. This also makes it easier to provide statistics and feedback to the legislators on efforts and impact.

The library organization may want to host webinars, create step-by-step guides and infographics, and have an informational page to assist schools, libraries, and local governing bodies with the changes.

Recently, Texas librarians faced the implementation of HB 900 (2023), which requires *all* book vendors to rate as "sexually relevant" or "sexually explicit" (or not) *all* books they have previously sold or will sell in the future to any Texas schools or school libraries. Subsequently, the Texas Library Association offered a frequently updated FAQ sheet as the law's impact and the required library responses became clearer.[1] This FAQ sheet helped librarians, publishers, and distributors understand what they must do to comply with the law. This is an example of how providing implementation assistance to local stakeholders makes it clear that you are there to make it easy for them to meet a law's requirements, and that librarians are partners in all mutual endeavors.

Go Further Together

Legislative advocacy is a high-frustration, high-reward activity, and success is often incremental. A robust ecosystem of supportive and collaborative team members is the only way success is possible. Team members who understand the legislative processes, timelines, and constraints will play a significant role, as will those who can speak passionately and succinctly about the group's goals. Others will be strong organizers or effective morale boosters. Each team member brings different strengths to the table, forming a harmonious whole that moves the group forward.

Acknowledgments

I extend my heartfelt appreciation to WLA advocates Sarah Logan, Elizabeth Roberts, Ryan Grant, Jamie Moffett, Samantha Harris, Gavin Downing, Rickey Barnett, Craig Seasholes, Christie Kaaland, and many more for their tireless and collaborative efforts in championing school libraries in Washington state. Working alongside and learning from each of you has been an honor.

NOTE

1. Texas Library Association, "HB 900 Implementation FAQ," last modified July 2023, https://txla.org/wp-content/uploads/2023/07/HB-900 -Implementation-FAQs_TLA-7-2023.pdf.

10

ECOSYSTEM WARRIORS STAND TOGETHER FOR INTELLECTUAL FREEDOM

Barbara K. Stripling

A n ecosystem, in human terms, is characterized by inter- actions of individuals with others and with their environ- ment. Ecosystems are dynamic and responsive to changes in both the living and nonliving parts; every aspect of an ecosystem depends on every other aspect. Ecosystems in libraries are living systems that involve *breathing in* (focusing on shared values, listening, collaborating, responding to diverse perspectives, com- municating) and *breathing out* (external sharing of policies and strate- gies, advocating, building relationships, delivering unified messages).

Intellectual freedom is a core value of libraries, brought to life by li- brary workers, supporters, and users. In practical terms, intellectual freedom is not a dormant principle to be called upon only in challenging times. Rather, intellectual freedom is defined by the freedom to take ac- tion: to choose what to read and write, to access information in any for- mat equitably and privately, to pursue diverse perspectives and points of view, to learn independently, and to express ideas with voice and agency.

Given the fact that every library is already part of the library ecosystem locally and in a wider sense, existing ecosystems have a huge opportuni- ty to focus some energy on collaborative efforts to strengthen intellectual freedom policies and awareness, as well as to advocate widely about in- tellectual freedom as a central tenet of democracy. This focus will benefit all members of the ecosystem as well as their patrons, communities, and the broader society. The impacts of an intellectual freedom-based library ecosystem will be deep and far-reaching. Libraries that fully support intellectual freedom in their ethos and action will include and unite diverse voices, recognize the importance of teaching individuals to exercise their intellectual freedom rights, and strengthen communities and the democratic process. Some of the impacts that focusing on intellectual freedom can have will be discussed in the sections below.

Impact: Strengthening the Core Value of Intellectual Freedom Itself

The alarming rise in challenges to library materials and programs has caused many libraries to strengthen their commitment to intellectual freedom. Libraries are sharing their policies and procedures publicly to clarify to the ecosystem community their mission and their criteria for collection development, programming, instruction, and services. Libraries are communicating to their communities that the freedom to read, write, create, and express whatever they wish is essential to their way of life and their future.

Many libraries ensure that all their resources and services are guided by the values inherent in intellectual freedom by incorporating values statements into their own mission and policies. For example, the Austin (TX) Public Library's "Materials Selection Policy" explicitly includes the principles upon which the collection is built and maintained, one of which is intellectual freedom:

> The freedom to read, along with the freedom to hear and to view, is protected by the First Amendment to the Constitution of the United States. This freedom, essential to our democracy, will be upheld, supported, and defended in the selection and accessibility of all library materials. In this regard, the library upholds the principles of the American Library Association's Library Bill of Rights, Freedom to Read, Freedom to View, Statement on Labeling and Free Access to Libraries for Minors, as well as the Texas Library Association's Intellectual Freedom Statement and the Materials Selection Policy.[1]

The Seattle (WA) Public Library has developed an explicit connection to intellectual freedom in its mission to serve the community. The library regards intellectual freedom as the "cornerstone of all public libraries" and "the freedom to read and access information is everyone's right." Furthermore, the library has published on its website an intellectual freedom commitment to its patrons:

> We will help you find the information or resources you seek, regardless of your background, point of view or beliefs. People of any race, ethnicity, citizenship status, gender identity or age have free access to Library materials and resources.[2]

Libraries are supported in their stance on intellectual freedom by an intellectual freedom ecosystem that extends nationally and incorporates several organizations, both within and outside of the library world, including the American Library Association, the Freedom to Read Foundation, the National Coalition Against Censorship, the Comic Book Legal Defense Fund, the Banned Books Week Coalition, and PEN.

Impact: Including and Unifying Diverse Voices

A second impact of focusing on intellectual freedom is the inclusion and unification of diverse voices. Individual libraries stand for intellectual freedom and build local ecosystems by including diverse voices through their collection development, programming, instruction, and services. For example, Lafayette College in Easton, Pennsylvania, explicitly publicizes its values of diversity, equity, and inclusion by the following practices: "Ensuring equity of access to information; Creating spaces and collections, and implementing services, that are inclusive and welcoming to all; Representing the diversity of our campus, local, and regional communities; Teaching students to be independent researchers and thinkers; Protecting the privacy of our users."[3]

The ecosystem supporting libraries' focus on inclusion and diversity has grown over the last few years to respond to the diversity of our communities and counter the marginalization of diverse voices. That support network includes authors, publishers, educators, young people, parents, decision-makers, rights and service organizations, and individual community members. Building an ecosystem that connects these diverse entities around the concept of intellectual freedom enables leaders to unite around a message, create a network of support, speak with *One Voice*, and influence decision-making and public policy. For example, Unite Against Book Bans, a national organization founded by the American Library Association, has garnered a wide array of partners (national, state, and local) and built an inclusive and extensive ecosystem to fight against censorship.[4]

Impact: Increased Recognition of the Skills, Attitudes, Responsibilities, and Actions Needed for Intellectual Freedom

Perhaps the most important impact of building a strong intellectual freedom-based library ecosystem is that it enables educators, decision-makers, and legislators to join with library staff and supporters in recognizing the importance of teaching intellectual freedom skills, attitudes, responsibilities, and actions if we hope to maintain a democratic and informed society.

In August 2021, local lawmakers in the District of Columbia (DC) demonstrated their understanding that school libraries are integral to the instructional programs in schools. They surprisingly dedicated $3,250,000 from the enrollment reserve to pay for librarians to be hired for the 2022 school year in the 36 DC schools that did not have one. This decision was made at least partly in response to advocacy by community members and librarians. The 2023–2024 DC Public Schools budget places the funding of libraries at Level 1 (no flexibility) and requires all schools to have at least a 1.0 librarian who is responsible for teaching research skills, digital citizenship, and information literacy strategies and for nurturing a culture of reading and engagement.[5]

Librarians in all types of libraries are increasingly recognizing the need to teach information-seekers how to determine the credibility and perspective of information, especially in the digital environment. Some have chosen to focus on the digital environment subset of intellectual freedom skills by focusing their curriculums on what is often called "media literacy."

Two examples illustrate the focus on media literacy for both public and school libraries:

- The Pitkin County Library (Aspen, CO) includes an extensive section on its website about intellectual freedom and the importance of critical-thinking skills in media literacy.[6]
- In November 2022, New Jersey became the first state to pass bipartisan legislation mandating information literacy education for all K-12 students.[7]

Impact: Strengthening Communities and the Democratic Process

Finally, the broadest impact of building a library ecosystem focused on intellectual freedom is on society itself. Communities are, by their very nature, comprised of diverse people, occupations, attitudes, cultures, and perspectives. With that diversity come challenges and inequities in income, education, and opportunities. An ecosystem focused on intellectual freedom has the potential to both celebrate diversity and address inequities. When that ecosystem is in place, it facilitates the sharing of strategies and best practices, relieves the isolation that librarians experience in facing challenges alone, and enables community members to gain the information and agency needed to participate in the democratic process. The two examples below provide a glimpse into the many ways that a focus on intellectual freedom and equity by libraries can result in strengthened communities.

Addressing Inequities

Funding from the Institute of Museum and Library Services (IMLS) has enabled libraries of all types across the country to develop strong local initiatives to address inequities and share their tools and solutions with the broader ecosystem of libraries. One example of an effective tool that resulted from IMLS funding is the "Toward Gigabit Libraries Toolkit," which was developed and revised by Internet2 and its Community Anchor Program to enable libraries to advocate for improved broadband connections for their communities (and thus greater intellectual freedom).[8]

Community-Building

Libraries of all types serve as community centers, or "third spaces"—safe spaces that are neither the home nor the school or office. In these spaces, individuals have the freedom to explore their own identities, learn about others in the community who are not like them, develop empathy and respect for differences, seek information about their own interests, and engage in the interchange of ideas and opinions. In other words, libraries serve as havens for intellectual freedom. In the past few years, a number of ALA presidents have selected community-building through libraries as their presidential focus. ALA has developed a series of posters to enumerate the reasons why libraries are powerful community builders. Many of those reasons focus on aspects of intellectual freedom:[9]

- Because libraries are hubs for civic engagement
- Because libraries promote justice and inclusion for all
- Because libraries bring people of all backgrounds together
- Because libraries let everyone's voice be heard
- Because libraries support those who need it most
- Because being together makes us stronger
- Because libraries give everyone a seat at the table

The current political divisiveness in communities across the country is severely threatening the intellectual freedom library ecosystem. Local and national campaigns have been organized to ban books from school libraries and challenge the professional decisions of librarians. This culture of blaming and banning has eroded trust in a fundamental principle of libraries—intellectual freedom—and precluded the intellectual freedom rights of some members of our society, particularly those from marginalized groups. These efforts are the antithesis of the community-building attributes of the library ecosystem listed above. Some libraries and librarians are having to fight for their very existence. The need for a strong intellectual freedom-based library ecosystem has never been more critical.

Building and Sustaining an Intellectual Freedom-Based Library Ecosystem

As illustrated above, the impacts of focusing on intellectual freedom as a foundation for a library ecosystem can be profound. In order to build and sustain such an ecosystem, library workers and supporters need to consider three main aspects or areas: (1) a shared and deep understanding of what intellectual freedom in libraries demands; (2) library practices (both internal and external) that promote intellectual freedom; and (3) policies and laws (both internal and external) that undergird the implementation of intellectual freedom practices. Each of these important areas is treated in the sections that follow.

Understanding Intellectual Freedom Demands

Intellectual freedom is easily defined in broad, conceptual language and platitudes (First Amendment rights, freedom of expression, freedom to read, equitable access to information), but its actual meaning for libraries and society is more nuanced. Intellectual freedom concepts must be translated into reality through the daily actions of all those who work in and support libraries. Implementing an intellectual freedom-based ecosystem depends on everyone in the library community, not just the leadership, making decisions and taking actions that bring intellectual freedom to life every day through maintaining the library's collection; planning and conducting instruction and programming events; interacting with patrons; and even managing the physical library space.

Some aspects of this implementation, however, are still being defined. For example, for many years, librarians considered their libraries "neutral" in providing equitable access to information because library collections were consciously built to include "all" opposing points of view. The neutrality of libraries has been challenged, however, by the recognition that "neutrality" is a false flag that hides the nuanced decision-making demanded of librarians. The 2018 ALA Midwinter President's Program "Are Libraries Neutral?" featured eight library professionals who presented opposing views of the concept of library and librarian neutrality.[10] Emily Knox presented a strong argument that library neutrality is a myth and librarians who believe in intellectual freedom must forego neutrality to stand up for their communities:

> Libraries, any library, cannot presume to be a hub for a community by being neutral. If libraries are about people, then they must take people's lives seriously. Even when supporting those lives might court some controversy. Deciding not to support marginalized people is never neutral. It is always a choice.[11]

Librarians who recognize that libraries are not neutral, but who are still driven by an intellectual freedom stance, now develop their collections by intentionally connecting to the diversity of their communities and building their collections and services to reflect diverse perspectives.

Some library workers are also engaged in trying to articulate the congruences and differences between social justice and intellectual freedom. Although intellectual freedom certainly encompasses attention to diversity, equity, and inclusion, its predominant focus is on the rights inherent in the freedom to read and express. Library workers can, and should, be warriors for equitable access to information, but warriors in their professional capacity, not for specific social justice causes. Drawing the line between personal passions and professional responsibilities is difficult but necessary if the ecosystem is to be inclusive of the perspectives of all members. The way to build a strong ecosystem is to focus on the shared values and actions inherent in intellectual freedom.

Library Practice

Once a solid understanding of intellectual freedom has been developed, a second area of building and supporting a library ecosystem based on intellectual freedom must be considered: *practice*. Ecosystems of library practice can be developed at different levels, from *internal* (within the organization itself or limited to one type of library) to *external* (community-wide, across multiple types of libraries, statewide, national).

For an ecosystem to flourish and have a measurable impact on individual libraries, the ecosystem must be nurtured first within each library itself (the *internal ecosystem*). An internal ecosystem can be built around the collection, the instructional program, programs and services, collaboration and communication, and the culture of the library. Each of those areas is strengthened when a larger, external ecosystem exists.

Many of the internal practices of libraries are supported by the *external ecosystem*, which includes multiple library types and levels as well as the communities they serve. The external, community-based ecosystem must be continually nurtured and strengthened because, increasingly, it may present challenges rather than support to libraries and librarians that base their programs on the tenets of intellectual freedom. State legislators, school administrators, and school and public library board members may have an agenda that enables them to ignore or overturn policies and procedures that guarantee the First Amendment rights of every member of the community.

An essential tool in thinking about the development of a statewide library ecosystem is the rubric prepared by a subcommittee of ALA's Committee on Library Advocacy, entitled "One Voice: A Continuum for Stronger Library Ecosystems." This rubric, fully discussed in chapter 3, offers specific guidance on state-level actions that can be taken in leadership, communication, collaboration, and sustainability to build an effective library ecosystem. Many of the elements in the rubric can be translated to both the local and national levels.

Collection Development

In terms of the selection and maintenance of the library collection with an intellectual freedom lens, several strategies might be employed. Front-line workers have the greatest opportunity to provide a rich picture of the diverse populations, identities, and preferences of the community being served. Collection-mapping to determine the accessibility of reading levels, languages, and formats can be conducted periodically. Thematic collection-mapping based on the following intellectual freedom themes can also be helpful:

- The diversity of cultures and languages represented in the collection
- The alignment of the collection with the needs and interests of the community
- The diversity and credibility of the perspectives included in the collection

Using circulation data to determine trends and patterns of use may provide some insights into the collection's appropriateness.

Collection development guided by intellectual freedom must not be based on a fear of controversy. The librarians who are reading reviews and making selections would be well-served to remember the axiom from librarian Jo Godwin, "A truly great library contains something in it to offend everyone."[12]

A vibrant external ecosystem supporting intellectual freedom in library collections has long been nurtured by ALA's Office for Intellectual Freedom through its collection and publication of data and trends and its support for librarians in responding to book challenges. With the almost exponential rise in censorship across the country over the last couple of years, the larger ecosystem has stepped up to counter these book-banning pressures. Rights organizations, professional associations, authors, publishers, librarians from every type of library, and members of the public have stood up and publicly defended intellectual freedom rights for all members of the community. Special attention has been paid to those materials and populations that are most marginalized in society.

Instruction

A major factor of intellectual freedom in libraries is empowering individuals with the skills to exercise their rights in credible and responsible ways. Teaching those skills, either directly or indirectly, is an essential component of the librarian's role in all types of libraries, but especially in school and academic libraries. These skills should be taught throughout the years of schooling, using a continuum that builds the level of complexity from year to year. Several tools are available online to guide librarians in the selection of appropriate skills to teach so as to enable students to understand and practice those skills.

Some individual school librarians, school districts, academic librarians, and academic library systems have developed internal curricula that often include intellectual freedom components, although sometimes these curricula take a reductionist approach and include only intellectual property, plagiarism, and citation. The broader ecosystem of individuals and organizations concerned with information literacy, civic responsibility, digital citizenship, digital literacy, and intellectual freedom has provided tools and strategies to support individual librarians in developing comprehensive curricula. One such tool is the "Empire State Information Fluency Continuum" developed by librarians in New York City and made available online through a Creative Commons license. In this continuum, the sections especially useful for teaching the skills of intellectual freedom are those delineated under Anchor Standard II, Media Literacy and Anchor Standard III, Social and Civic Responsibility, as well as the lessons on Digital Citizenship.[13]

Because the realm of intellectual freedom skills and strategies is quite large, a librarian may choose to focus on a specific aspect of intellectual freedom instruction, like media literacy or digital citizenship. Many organizations and individuals offer toolkits, sample lessons, and guidance in these areas. Examples of resources on media literacy include those offered by the Center for Media Literacy, the National Association for Media Literacy Education (NAMLE), Project Look Sharp, and the News Literacy Project. Examples of resources on digital citizenship include those offered by Common Sense Education, the International Society for Technology in Education (ISTE), and the University of Washington's Center for an Informed Public.[14] The national ecosystems around media literacy and digital citizenship are vibrant and continue to evolve.

Programs and Services

Decisions about a library's programs and services tend to be made at the individual library or perhaps the library system level. By building a strong intellectual freedom ecosystem within the library, decisions to offer programming and services that acknowledge and support marginalized groups or individuals in the community are understood and supported by other members of the library staff. If those decisions are challenged by other members of the community, the library is able to articulate a unified response, and provide a rationale for the choices and decisions made. The internal ecosystem's support enables librarians and libraries to summon the courage to offer programming and services that transform their libraries from simply "safe" spaces to "brave" spaces.

Internal decision-making on programs and services is not unaffected by the external library ecosystem, particularly when it comes to controversial areas concerning intellectual freedom. Certainly, libraries can garner ideas and support from the experiences of other libraries and enhance their own programming and services as a result. Care must be taken, though, to adopt and adapt only those practices that are firmly grounded in their value to the local community. For example, drag queen story hours have trended across the country and have proven to be highly successful in motivating young children to read, but they are controversial in some communities that do not understand the rationale. Librarians will be better able to defend their programming decisions if they have developed a strong intellectual freedom argument beforehand.

Collaboration and Communication

Collaboration and communication operate synergistically. Wider communication leads to increased opportunities for collaboration; and successful collaboration communicates shared values more effectively than simply sending messages. Every ecosystem depends on both collaboration and communication to be effective.

Relationships are built around shared values. Since intellectual freedom is widely shared as a foundational value for libraries and library workers, it opens the doors to collaboration. When librarians from all library types recognize their mutual interest in intellectual freedom-related issues, like offering access to diverse collections, they can collaborate to build systems and share resources that cross library types and enhance each participating member. Special events featuring controversial issues or authors can be developed and delivered collaboratively. Best practices in instruction, community engagement, the use of space, and equitable access can be shared among colleagues who offer rich perspectives from different types of libraries. Examples of this interlibrary collaboration and adaptation can be found across the country.

Effective communication can be developed as a result of ecosystem collaboration, or it can actually power the development of an ecosystem. In New York City, for example, Melissa Jacobs started a discussion list (NYCSLIST) among school librarians in 2004 that has since grown to over 1,000 subscribers. NYCSLIST started as a communication tool to enable librarians to share their practices in a collaborative way, and it has now become an important component in building a culture and ecosystem among school librarians in New York City. Librarians learn from each other, share their best ideas, ask and answer each other's questions, and develop relationships that are cemented when the librarians actually get the opportunity to meet their fellow librarians in person.[15]

Communication can also be used as an advocacy tool. When it comes to intellectual freedom, speaking with *One Voice* is absolutely essential. The messages to the field, the public, and decision-makers are vital to show a united library front and deliver the rationale for changes that need to be made to ensure that every member of the community (local, state, and national) is supported in their right to read, express, and access information.

These advocacy efforts are often led by members of the larger library ecosystem. Legislative committees from the American Library Association and state library associations develop yearly agendas and host advocacy days to foster relationship-building between library supporters and legislators. Individuals may also be influential. Carolyn Foote, a retired school librarian from Texas, co-founded a national movement called FReadom Fighters to counter the increased incidents of book banning.[16]

Nonprofit organizations and professional associations have been particularly active in their support of intellectual freedom and libraries. PEN America was founded in 1922 to champion the freedom to write. The organization offers data, research, webinars, events, and nationwide advocacy in support of intellectual freedom topics of high concern, including book bans, educational censorship, campus free speech, disinformation, and online abuse.[17] The Comic Book Legal Defense Fund offers numerous library and educator tools to combat the censorship of graphic novels and nonfiction and protect the rights of the comic art form and its community of readers, librarians, publishers, and retailers.[18]

Library Policies, Regulations, and Strategic Advocacy

The third main area to consider in building and sustaining an intellectual freedom-based library ecosystem is library policies, regulations, and strategic advocacy. Although every library, school district, and library system has developed a broad range of policies for the management and operation of the library within the guidelines of local and state regulations, four specific policies are most important for ensuring the First Amendment rights of all constituents: collection development, challenged materials, privacy, and equitable access. All policies must be approved by the governing body of the institution and, ideally, developed collaboratively.

Collection Development (Materials Selection) Policies

A library's collection development or materials selection policy may be the most important venue for establishing the intellectual freedom context and getting official approval of that stance. The best policies include statements of the values that underlie the library program, either using local phrasing or including wording from the First Amendment or key American Library Association values documents (e.g., ALA's Library Bill of Rights, The Freedom to Read, the Freedom to View Statement, and Free Access to Libraries for Minors).[19]

In the last few years, many libraries and library systems have updated their policies to explicitly include the concepts of diversity and inclusion as criteria for the selection of new materials. The Naperville (IL) Public Library's Board of Directors issued a Diversity Statement in the summer of 2020 outlining the library's support for diversity, equity, and inclusion and offering specific examples of intellectual freedom practices in the library.[20]

- Supporting the intellectual freedom for everyone to read and view materials of their choice, and resisting calls to censor materials and viewpoints;
- Offering reading recommendations relevant to our diverse community, including, but not limited to, diversity, racial justice, equity, race, religion, ability, gender, and sexuality; and
- Providing varied programs, including storytimes in multiple languages, and cultural and historical events for adults.

Following the adoption of the Diversity Statement, the Naperville Public Library's material selections policy was revised in February 2021. It includes a section on intellectual freedom with the following statement: "The Library has the responsibility to provide materials representing a wide range of ideas and opinions, including controversial, unpopular, and unorthodox viewpoints and expression."[21]

School libraries, which often face the brunt of challenges to library materials, have developed materials selection policies that explicitly mention intellectual freedom and access to diverse materials. The Monroe (GA) Area High School's materials selection policy explains the school's position on intellectual freedom ("Materials should reflect a variety of formats as well as cultural diversity and the pluralistic nature of contemporary American society") as well as its criteria for the selection of library materials, three of which apply specifically to the access, diversity, and inclusion aspects of intellectual freedom.[22]

- Reflective of the pluralistic nature of a global society: Library media materials should provide a global perspective and promote diversity as a positive attribute of our society. It is important to include materials by authors and illustrators of all cultures.
- Free of bias and stereotypes: Materials should reflect the basic humanity of all people and should be free of stereotypes, caricatures, distorted dialect, sexual bias, and other offensive characteristics. Library materials concerning religious, social, and political content should inform rather than indoctrinate.
- Representative of differing viewpoints on controversial subjects: Students have the right to information on both sides of a controversial issue. By having access to a variety of resources, students will have the knowledge base to develop critical thinking and problem-solving skills.

Challenged Materials Policies

Challenged materials policies are generally included as part of materials selection policies. Typically, they describe the process to follow when a material is challenged, and link to a form that the challenger must complete to initiate the review process. The Chicago Public Schools adopted a revised materials selection policy that included a challenged materials procedure in February 2022.[23] The policy outlines a procedure for reviewing challenges, a model process that has been widely accepted by the library ecosystem, even in this time of increasing challenges:

- Engage in a conversation with the challenger to clarify the issues, present the library stance on intellectual freedom and the right to equitable access, and outline the challenge process.
- If the issue cannot be resolved in the informal meeting, the complainant is offered a copy of the complaint form which must be completed before the complaint can proceed. The form includes key questions about the complainant's reasoning: what is the specific objection; did the complainant read the entire work, or, if not, what parts were read; how the complainant thinks students will be impacted; whether the complainant knows of any evaluations or reviews of the material; what value is there in the material; and what actions would the complainant wish to be taken.
- Once the complaint is submitted (must be completed within two weeks), the librarian, teacher, or principal notifies the central office libraries team, who will form a review committee and consider the material (in its entirety) carefully within two weeks. The committee will deliberate and decide if the material meets the criteria established in the collection development policy.
- The written decision of the review committee will be sent to the complainant who has the right to appeal the decision to the libraries team supervisor who will consult with the Chief Officer of Teaching and Learning and issue a final decision.
- The material will remain in the library during the entire review process.

Although challenges are handled at the local level, school boards and boards of directors can be reassured that the approved materials selection policy carefully outlines the procedure to follow for challenges and that the larger library ecosystem has accepted the legitimacy of the model process as outlined above.

Privacy Policies

The third policy area is privacy. In June 2019, the Council of the American Library Association approved a revision to its policy statement "Privacy: An Interpretation of the Library Bill of Rights." The interpretation states clearly that the privacy of a patron's open inquiry and the confidentiality of patrons' records are "essential to the exercise of free speech, free thought, and free association" and are integral to the library's mission.[24] Through the leadership of ALA, a national ecosystem supporting the right to privacy and confidentiality is firmly in place.[25]

Technology has presented new challenges to maintaining patrons' privacy rights. ALA has published "Library Privacy Guidelines for Learning Management Systems" (revised as recently as April 2022) to empower individual libraries and library systems to employ appropriate data management and security practices in order to secure patron privacy.[26] Even though the ethical position is to erase patron checkout and personally identifiable data, librarians may be caught between patrons' wishes and this ethical stance. Some patrons request that the library maintain their reading records to ease their selection of new reading materials. Librarians can respond by helping patrons develop alternate ways to capture their own use of library materials.

Interactive library websites and the widespread use of social media also challenge libraries' commitment to the personal privacy and confidentiality of their patrons. When a library site is opened to public comment, the danger is that patrons themselves will post personal information on it. As a result, libraries have, in large part, shut off interactivity in both their websites and their social media accounts. What seems like a less engaging approach to library services is actually a positive strategy to preserve patrons' privacy.

Equitable Access Policies

Providing equitable access (especially to the digital environment) continues to be a problematic area for most libraries, although some national initiatives are addressing the problem. An assessment of people's basic facility with technological devices and platforms has revealed a generation gap that many libraries are trying to address through instruction and support for all ages. Beyond technological expertise, there is a growing crisis in the lack of skills and motivation to critically analyze and select credible information available online. Many users, both youth and adults, are swayed by disinformation, biased information, and politically motivated messages. Libraries have shifted their instructional programs to address the need of both adults and youth to learn the thinking skills behind successful digital information searching and sharing.

Other issues of equitable access are not so easily addressed. In many areas of the country, especially in rural and isolated areas, high-speed broadband is not available. Even when broadband has been expanded to rural hubs, many households live in that "last mile" and do not have connections from the hubs to their own homes. Certainly, smartphones have alleviated some of this lack of access, but smartphones limit the depth of information finding and producing. Librarians have tackled the political and civic ecosystems and lobbied them to bring broadband access to a priority level in their communities.

Librarians are aware of the limitations to equitable access posed by patrons' physical or mental issues, languages, and out-of-the-mainstream interests and identities. Librarians have responded by using the principles of universal design to develop support materials and create accessible library spaces. In terms of collection development and the offering of specialized services, however, most libraries are operating with limited funding. As a result, they have difficulty filling the gaps for these populations so as to provide greater equity of access. National support from grants and foundations sometimes provides the needed funds. Some librarians have assumed entrepreneurship as part of their job description.

Equitable access to e-books and e-textbooks is a problem for all types of libraries. The library community continues to work within the broader ecosystem of software providers, publishers, librarians, library systems, and networks to build diverse e-book collections and to achieve balanced lending models for libraries.

Regulations and Strategic Advocacy

Library policies and practices must operate within regulations set by law (both state and federal) and by decision-makers and agencies at all levels who may make decisions that are antithetical to intellectual freedom in libraries. Lawmakers and regulators are influenced by public pressure. Unfortunately, the current political climate in the country and the very strong advocacy by certain groups who favor censorship have resulted in decisions by school and library boards to withdraw materials from library collections and forbid programming and displays on certain topics (e.g., race, gender identity, homosexuality). Template legislation to censor library materials on those same issues has been shared with state legislators across the country, and some of that legislation has already been enacted.

In July 2022, Florida's controversial "Parental Rights in Education" bill (HB 1557), dubbed by opponents as the "Don't Say Gay" bill, went into effect. The bill bans instruction on gender identity and sexual orientation to children from kindergarten through grade 3. Some Florida school districts have already removed some books with LGBTQ themes from their school libraries. The Florida Department of Education has developed a mandated training for school librarians about their book selection process under House Bill 1467, and as of July 1, 2023, districts must certify that all school librarians and media specialists have completed the online training.[27] The training outlines the materials prohibited by the state law under the state's definition of "harmful to minors." The shift to parental rights is explicitly stated in one of the criteria for "harmful to minors": "Is patently offensive to prevailing standards in the adult community as a whole with respect to what is suitable material or conduct for minors." These types of laws have the potential to spread nationally.

Other bills that restrict intellectual freedom in libraries are being introduced, deliberated, and in some cases, passed in state legislatures. The Freedom to Read Foundation[28] keeps a close watch on federal and state legislation and provides support to local and state advocacy groups.

The need for strong intellectual freedom-based library ecosystem advocacy has probably never been greater.

One bright spot in terms of strategic advocacy has been offered by the American Library Association with its workshop and white paper on digital inclusion and broadband. The report, entitled "Leverage Libraries to Achieve Digital Equity for All," lays out a strategic plan for the use of federal funding under the Infrastructure Investment and Jobs Act, as well as federal agencies and resources, to "accelerate broadband adoption and skills building for all nationwide."[29]

Final Thoughts: Warrior Leadership

A new type of leadership is required to build and sustain an intellectual freedom-based library ecosystem, one that collaborates and builds relationships across library types, aligned organizations, and communities. One that breaks through political and social barriers to avert crises before they happen. One that offers both strategic and emotional support to librarians and libraries facing challenges. One that seeks diverse perspectives and enables the ecosystem community to find common ground and speak with one voice. We need leaders who are warriors for intellectual freedom, who are willing to take risks and act as change agents to ensure that the right to read, view, create, and share information is guaranteed for every member of the community. The time is now.

NOTES

1. Austin Public Library, "Materials Selection Policy," https://library.austin texas.gov/about-library/materials-selection-policy.
2. Seattle Public Library, "Intellectual Freedom," www.spl.org/programs-and -services/social-justice/intellectual-freedom.
3. Lafayette College, "Library Mission and Values Statements," https://library .lafayette.edu/about/library-mission-and-values-statements/.
4. American Library Association, "Unite Against Book Bans," https:// uniteagainstbookbans.org/.
5. DC Public Schools, "Building a Budget with Allocations—All Flexibility Levels Level 1 Flexibility Allocations," https://dcpsbudget.com/budget -development-guide/level-1-flexibility-allocations/.
6. Pitkin County Library, "Intellectual Freedom," https://pitcolib.org/visit/ library-services-resources/intellectual-freedom.
7. New Jersey Education Association, "Gov. Murphy Signs Bipartisan Legislation Establishing Information Literacy Education," www.njea.org/ gov-murphy-signs-bipartisan-legislationestablishing-information-literacy -education/.
8. Internet2, "Toward Gigabit Libraries," https://internet2.edu/community/ community-anchor-program/cap-library-resources/toward-gigabit -libraries/; Greg Landgraf, "The Last Mile: Toolkit Enables Libraries to Advocate for Their Broadband Connections," *American Libraries*, March 1, 2022, https://americanlibrariesmagazine.org/2022/03/01/the-last-mile/.

9. American Library Association, "Libraries = Strong Communities Toolkit," I Love Libraries, https://ilovelibraries.org/librariestransform/libraries -strong-communities/.

10. American Libraries staff, "Are Libraries Neutral? Highlights from the Midwinter President's Program," *American Libraries*, June 1, 2018, https://americanlibrariesmagazine.org/2018/06/01/are-libraries-neutral/.

11. Emily Knox, "Remarks from ALA Midwinter 2018 President's Program," www.emilyknox.net/midwinter-2018-remarks.

12. Krissa Corbett Cavouras, Season 1, episode 3, "Episode Transcript," April 9, 2019, in *Something to Offend Everyone*, podcast, audio transcript, 22:20, www.bklynlibrary.org/podcasts/something-offend-everyone. Bianca Hezekiah is a young adult librarian at the Eastern Parkway branch (of the Brooklyn Public Library).

13. Barbara K. Stripling, "Empire State Information Literacy Continuum," https://slsa-nys.libguides.com/ifc/continuum; New York City Public Schools, "New York City School Library System Homepage/Digital Citizen ship," NYCDOE LibGuide, https://nycdoe.libguides.com/digitalcitizenship.

14. National Association for Media Literacy Education (NAMLE), "Learn How to Access, Analyze, Evaluate, Create, and Act Using All Forms of Communication," https://namle.net/resources/; Ithaca College, "Search Our Extensive Collection of Free Media Literacy Lessons and PD Resources," Project Look Sharp, https://projectlooksharp.org/index.php; News Literacy Project, "NewsLitNation Forum for Educators," https://newslit.org/newslit-nation/#tools; Common Sense Education, "Everything You Need to Teach Digital Citizenship," www.commonsense.org/education/digital -citizenship; ISTE, "Digital Citizenship in Education," www.iste.org/areas-of-focus/digital-citizenship; Center for an Informed Public, "Resources," www.cip.uw.edu/resources/.

15. Susan Brown Faghani, "List Owner Insights: How NYCSLIST Became the Go-to Resource for New York City School Librarians," L-Soft, www.lsoft .com/news/nycslist-issue2-2016.asp.

16. Megan McGibney, "74 Interview: FReadom Fighters Co-Founder Carolyn Foote on Why School Librarians Matter as Book Bans Rock the Country," The 74, www.the74million.org/article/74-interview-freedom-fighters -co-founder-carolyn-foote-on-why-school-librarians-matter-as-book -bans-rock-the-country/.

17. PEN America, "Book Bans," https://pen.org/issue/book-bans/#.

18. Jeff Trexler, "CBLDF @ NYCC," CBLDF (Comic Book Legal Defense Fund), https://cbldf.org.

19. American Library Association, "Library Bill of Rights," www.ala.org/advocacy/intfreedom/librarybill; "The Freedom to Read Statement," www.ala.org/advocacy/intfreedom/freedomreadstatement; "The Freedom to View," www.ala.org/advocacy/intfreedom/freedomviewstatement; "Access to Library Resources and Services for Minors: An Interpretation of the Library Bill of Rights," www.ala.org/advocacy/intfreedom/librarybill/interpretations/minors.

20. Naperville Public Library, "Board of Trustees Diversity Statement," www.naperville-lib.org/195/Board-of-Trustees-Diversity-Statement.

21. Naperville Public Library, "Naperville PL Materials Selection Policy," www.naperville-lib.org/DocumentCenter/View/250/Materials-Selection-Policy-PDF.

22. Monroe Area High School, "MAHS Selection Policy," www.walton.k12.ga.us/MAHSSelectionPolicy.aspx.

23. Chicago Public Schools, "Collection Development," www.cps.edu/sites/cps-policy-rules/policies/600/604/604-7/.

24. American Library Association, "Privacy: An Interpretation of the Library Bill of Rights," www.ala.org/advocacy/intfreedom/librarybill/interpretations/privacy#.

25. American Library Association, "Privacy."

26. American Library Association, "Library Privacy Guidelines for Library Management Systems," www.ala.org/advocacy/privacy/guidelines/library-management-systems.

27. Florida Department of Education, www.fldoe.org/core/fileparse.php/20562/urlt/8-6.pdf.

28. Freedom to Read Foundation, www.ftrf.org.

29. American Library Association, "Leverage Libraries to Achieve Digital Equity for All: New Federal Funding Can Power Progress," www.ala.org/sites/default/files/advocacy/content/telecom/broadband/Digital_Equity_Report_Exec_Summary_102022.pdf.

PART IV
Many Kinds of Library Advocates

11

ACADEMIC LIBRARIES NEED THE LIBRARY ECOSYSTEM

Rachel Minkin and Jennifer Dean

cademic libraries have a critical place in the overarching library ecosystem. Academic libraries serve institutions of higher education: community colleges, four-year colleges, and advanced degree-granting universities. Within the latter two groups, institutions are classified in various ways: as regional comprehensive institutions that offer an array of programs to students in their regions; as liberal arts institutions that focus on a core set of courses and principles; and as research institutions, which are further split into types according to their degree of research output.[1] Although this statement may seem obvious, there is a world of difference between these institution types, and therefore, there is a world of difference in how these libraries work with external partners. External partners include library organizations and other types of libraries within the relevant states and regions. External partners also include vendors, publishers, disciplinary societies (history, science, etc.), and other academic colleagues within the institutions themselves, not to mention grant-supporting foundations and government entities. These relationships are different for each type of academic library, with a flagship research institution more likely to be focused at a regional and national level, while a community college is more likely to be focused on its internal institutional partners.[2] Community colleges also often have strong ties to the local K–12 systems, especially around dual-credit course offerings.

Unveiling the Current Landscape of Academic Libraries

Competition for resources, cuts to budgets, and concern about the roles of libraries and library workers is a part of life for libraries of all types. Academic libraries cannot claim any special privileges in this regard. However, it is useful to understand the current environment for academic libraries.

A brief perusal of local and trade news outlets highlights a decline in public opinion regarding the importance of a college degree, in addition to ongoing resource competition between higher ed institutions.[3] This competition results from lower levels of federal and state support, declining enrollments due to demographic changes, and changes resulting from the COVID-19 pandemic. By its very nature, each college or university is competing with other colleges and universities for a finite number of students in any given year. As crass as this may seem, the truth is that these students equate to the financial resources available within an institution. In addition to actual tuition dollars, student enrollment may also be tied to state and federal funding.

This competition for resources among our parent institutions affects their libraries, too. From a higher education administrator's standpoint, the mission and organization of the modern library is not generally well understood, much less the external context within which academic libraries operate. Academic libraries command large budgets and large staffs when compared with other academic support units; but continuously rising inflation in the cost of academic materials (whether print or digital) can make academic library collections budgets an attractive place to look for cuts. The funding for academic libraries, although not necessarily tied to student enrollment directly, is at the whim of the finances of the larger institution and as such, academic library resources are finely balanced between what belongs to the institution and what is shareable.

Academic libraries are in fact living in multiple ecosystems: our library ecosystem, the higher education ecosystem, and the institutional ecosystem.

A Call to Advocacy for Academic Libraries

The need to advocate for academic libraries both internally and externally is growing, and we need our friends in school and public libraries to join us.

> Having "non-librarian" allies who speak up for the importance of libraries is good, but it is not enough. To be successful, advocacy must be a full-time and consciously proactive behavior pattern in the library profession.
>
> To grab our fair share of the financial resources and to establish and maintain credibility in the broader academic community, librarians must learn to effectively market and advertise library services.[4]

Like our colleague libraries, collaboration is built into academic library work, both cross-departmentally within the university, and with similar institutions; many libraries have collaboration for the benefit of academic goals built into their mission. Academic library leadership is encouraged to develop relationships with the library's external community, most often in fundraising and grant projects. The university manages marketing, public affairs, and political advocacy while billing departments, including the library, for these services. Most academic library leaders are specifically discouraged from communicating with political leadership unless they are engaged by the university's governmental relations staff. That said, library staff may collaborate on advocacy projects with librarians from other institutions and library types, but under controlled circumstances. And of course, library staff remain citizens with personal rights to speak on behalf of all libraries.

A recent study of community college libraries indicates that these librarians do see their libraries as part of an ecosystem.[5] In the context of this report, "ecosystem" refers to the libraries' relationship to other units in their institutions. Though the results of that study cannot be extrapolated to other types of academic institutions without further research, the executive findings seemed plausible for us when viewed in the context of our research and regional comprehensive institutions, respectively. At this point in time, academic libraries are focused on internal collaborations. Student success is paramount. Our time is spent developing relationships and integrating our personnel and services with student academic support entities, such as student success and writing centers. The community college study also found that community college library directors expected external partnerships—including those with public libraries—to remain stable. The types of partnerships celebrated in ALA's Ecosystem Initiative are important at institutions like ours, but we do not believe academic libraries, or their parent institutions, will make these partnerships a priority unless they can be tied directly to recruitment, retention, or student success.[6]

Student Success in Higher Ed Is a Top Priority

Student success in higher education requires students to understand what libraries are, how library resources and staff can facilitate their individual academic success, and how to use the library. This sentence implies that these students graduate from K-12 schools with some awareness of the benefits they accrued from their K-12 libraries; university librarians should care that K-12 schools have strong library programs.

The ecosystem *could* directly impact student success beyond K-12. "First Years Meet the Frames" is a 2022 study of students just entering New Jersey colleges.[7] The study considered "the value of certified school librarians in providing resources and instruction to bridge situations of inequity and information poverty and identify gaps relating to academic preparedness among first-year students in New Jersey colleges." They surveyed high school librarians "to identify instructional strategies, resources and professional preparedness in programs identified by the New Jersey School Library Association (NJASL) as effective." They also followed the graduates of "high schools with effective school library programs into the spring of their college freshman year to uncover their levels of confidence and competence with academic research and to identify gaps that might need to be addressed in K12 library programs." The resulting data offers many insights into how K-12 and academic libraries are interrelated and would do well to collaborate on advocacy focused on ensuring that K-20 students maintain consistent access to strong library programming led by certified and degreed library staff. There is also a new toolkit put out by the Association of College & Research Libraries, the "Academic Library Advocacy Toolkit: Student Success Toolkit," which offers many resources to support improving campus-wide awareness of library impacts on student success.[8]

But academic librarians have not yet given the concept of a library ecosystem any particular focus. Given the myriad of challenges facing those academic libraries, an ecosystem initiative is unlikely to rise to the top of their concerns anytime soon. However, considering the conundrum that student success beyond K-12 is more likely when students come to higher ed familiar with what libraries are and do, academic librarians would be well-served to reconsider the merits of ecosystem thinking and work.

Data Can Prove the Value of the Library

Academic librarians and libraries generally value the insights gathered through research, data, and benchmarking. This is built into our DNA. We know that academic libraries are part of an academic institution's reason for being and have been so for a very long time. As the proverbial "heart of the campus," our libraries were not expected to prove their worth. And so even as the world of academia changed, we did not take cues from other library types about the need to market our contributions to our educational setting. Academic libraries have been able to function for a long time without examining their work as it is related to creating value for their institutions and the students they serve. With the continued development of online resources and remote learning, however, coupled with resource scarcity, academic libraries now must find ways to directly connect the work they do to the success of their students and the value of their institutions. *The Value of Academic Libraries* (2010), often referred to as "the VAL report," marked the start of the ACRL's and academic libraries' use of comprehensive data in making a case for the continued funding and support of academic libraries.[9] The VAL report has significantly shaped the work of the ACRL and its member libraries to this day, and has led to research, professional development, grants, and outreach in assessment, impact, and data analytics. "Project Outcome for Academic Libraries" is an ongoing element of the ACRL's Value of Academic Libraries initiative. Based on a model developed by the Public Library Association, this free toolkit further demonstrates how academic libraries can learn from other library types how to build stronger internal advocacy, as well as how to join the library ecosystem.[10]

A Cautionary Tale

Although we know that intellectual freedom has served as a rallying point for libraries of all types and is especially salient now, we also know that challenges to intellectual freedom impact libraries differently. Academic librarians are unlikely to be on the front lines of book and content challenges in the way our school and public library colleagues are. That said, the example of Texas A&M University taking faculty status away from its librarians offers a motivation to develop our internal marketing programs quickly, so as to enlist strong awareness in our faculty colleagues that they need a strong library. Texas A&M's leadership was determined to reorganize its libraries and proceeded very quickly.[11] Alyson Vaaler comments, "I never imagined this happening here. But we are not the first ones this has happened to and probably won't be the last. The way that it happened was particularly messy, but there is a trend to phase out faculty librarians at universities."[12] This is ecosystem-relevant without being focused on intellectual freedom. Possibly, had the library community on campus and beyond been more proactive in keeping the A&M leadership aware of what the university libraries offer the system's campuses, the forced change could have been avoided.

Standing Together with Other Library Types

Appendix C, "A Comparison of Public, School, and Academic Libraries: Vital to Our Communities," offers a parallel illustration of the overlaps and differences between public, school, and academic libraries, and shows how these different library types build upon each other's work to leverage their unique strengths, and thus contribute to the whole.[13] Given that academic librarians face such strong competition for funding support within their institutions, they might begin to recognize that K-12 and public librarians could speak for them. Every degreed librarian in any library has appreciated and relied on the library at the university they attended and sees the continuing importance of those libraries. If an outcry is needed, academic libraries need to ask for help in amplifying their voices. There may be some advance need for broader marketing of the reasons why academic libraries should not continue to be ignored—

but this is the same battle librarians at all levels wage for recognition. And after years of not knowing this support was needed, it will take a bit of rabble-rousing to make the change.

Additionally, academic librarians rely on a steady stream of new students who have the library skills a college education requires. Even students who choose trade school will require core research skills to be able to locate the proper parts number for car repair or plumbing connections. Librarians know that the internet can never replace the skills librarians bring to student support and the research process. Academic librarians are also voting citizens able to write personal letters to legislators who hold sway over essential funding. These letters can support libraries across the ecosystem. We must all stand together as librarians and as citizens.

Overlapping Ecosystems Still Need One Library Voice

From an academic perspective, documenting narratives of the various fronts on which libraries of all types must raise community awareness creates opportunities for scholars to study such narratives and share strategies based on documented evidence. These data-based activities would fit with libraries'—and particularly academic libraries—focus on research and benchmarking and enable the library ecosystem to develop additional strategies and tools based on what is working. This is only one possible way that academic librarians might both solidify their own positions within the hierarchy of academia and contribute to the strength of the larger library ecosystem.

Academic librarians are working in a higher education ecosystem which takes much of their time and energy. Intellectual freedom is only one front on which librarians must fight, and the way that fight will look differs across library types and geographic regions. Knowing that our battles may be different, we can recognize that each type of librarian must face adversity as part of our day-to-day existence, for our very existence—for funding, for recognition, for professional rights—and this unifies us, whether the challenge comes from our community, our boards, or our administration. There is great value in bringing these stories to the forefront so that library workers of all types may develop a greater understanding of one another.

NOTES

1. J. R. Thelin, *A History of American Higher Education*, 3rd ed. (Baltimore, MD: Johns Hopkins University Press, 2019).

2. M. Blankstein, and C. Wolff-Eisenberg, "Library Strategy and Collaboration across the College Ecosystem: Results from a National Survey of Community College Library Directors," 2021, https://doi.org/10.18665/sr.315922.

3. F. Diep, "Can a National Marketing Campaign Change the Souring Conversation about College?" *Chronicle of Higher Education*, December 16, 2022, www.chronicle.com/article/can-a-national-marketing-campaign -change-the-souring-conversation-about-college; L. Gardner, "Flagships Prosper, while Regionals Suffer: Competition Is Getting Fierce, and the Gap Is Widening," *Chronicle of Higher Education*, February 13, 2023, www.chronicle.com/article/flagships-prosper-while-regionals-suffer; D. Jesse, "U-M Flint Hits Crossroads as Enrollment Slumps; Transformation Study Underway," *Detroit Free Press*, February 5, 2023, www.freep.com/ in-depth/news/education/2023/02/05/u-m-flint-hits-crossroads-as -enrollment-slumps-transformation-study-underway/69818143007/.

4. Terry Kirchner, "Advocacy 101 for Academic Librarians: Tips to Help Your Institution Prosper," *College & Research Libraries News*, 1999, https://crln .acrl.org/index.php/crlnews/article/view/20704/25302.

5. Blankstein and Wolff-Eisenberg, "Library Strategy and Collaboration."

6. American Library Association, "ONE VOICE: Building a Strong Library Ecosystem," 2023, www.ala.org/advocacy/ala-ecosystem-initiative; D. Hand and S. K. Johns, "One Voice: Building a Strong Library Ecosystem," ACRL Insider, April 2, 2021, https://acrl.ala.org/acrlinsider/one-voice-building -a-strong-library-ecosystem/.

7. Joyce Valenza et al., "First Years Meet the Frames," School of Communication and Information, Rutgers, the State University of New Jersey, 2022, https://comminfo.libguides.com/FirstYearsFrames/

8. Association of College & Research Libraries, "Academic Library Advocacy Toolkit: Student Success," https://acrl.libguides.com/advocacytoolkit/ studentsuccess.

9. Association of College & Research Libraries, *Value of Academic Libraries: A Comprehensive Research Review and Report* (Chicago: ACRL, 2010), https://acrl.ala.org/value/?page_id=21.

10. Association of College & Research Libraries, "Project Outcome: Measuring the True Outcome of Libraries," https://acrl.projectoutcome.org/.

11. Josh Moody, "Texas A&M Librarians Lose Tenure in Reorganization Plan," Inside Higher Ed, May 24, 2022, www.insidehighered.com/quicktakes/2022/05/25/texas-am-librarians-lose-tenure-reorganization-plan.

12. Alyson Vaaler, "Uncertain Times: Changing from a Faculty to Staff Librarian at Texas A&M (Guest Post)," *This Liaison Life: Adventures of an Embedded Business Librarian* (blog), August 16, 2022, https://liaisonlife.wordpress.com/2022/08/16/from-faculty-to-staff/.

13. American Library Association, Committee on Library Advocacy, Ecosystem Subcommittee, "A Comparison of Public, School, and Academic Libraries: Vital to Our Communities," www.ala.org/sites/default/files/advocacy/content/Ecosystem%20Public%2C%20School%20and%20Academic%20Libraries%20Fact%20Sheet_0.pdf.

12

SCHOOL LIBRARIES ARE PILLARS IN LIBRARY ECOSYSTEMS

Kathy Lester

O ur democratic society flourishes when literate citizens have equitable access to libraries throughout their lives regardless of age, geography, or any other potential barriers. Literacy is more than just reading words on a page; it includes understanding how to access, evaluate, and use information. Students who grow up with strong school libraries will probably be more successful in college and life, and will also be better prepared as citizens, voters, and leaders of their communities. The fact that students explore learning independently for the first time in school libraries contributes to the importance of K-12 library programs to the library ecosystem overall.

School librarians work with the entire school community and provide access, experiences, lessons, and opportunities to *every* student in their school. Students who attend a school with an effective school library staffed by a certified school librarian learn how to use the resources in that library under the tutelage of professional librarians. But this exposure is not enough to ensure lifelong library use; further advocacy will be important in retaining library awareness into adulthood. Remember the definition of the library ecosystem:

> The interconnected network of all types of libraries, library workers, volunteers, and associations that provide and facilitate library services for community members—families; K-20 learners;

college and university communities; local, state and federal legislatures and government offices; businesses; nonprofits; and other organizations with specific information needs.[1]

Public and academic library advocates need school librarians on the team just as much as K-12 librarians need to join the team.

Collaborating beyond the School Day

Student patrons are best served when school libraries and public libraries collaborate to promote and enhance their respective "in school" and "out of school" library services. Upper-level student patrons are well-served when they have easy access to local community college or university libraries as they transition to the world of higher education. Our patrons—all of them—need to understand the library ecosystem and how school, public, and academic libraries complement one another to ensure library services for every resident from infancy through adulthood.

In thinking about the interconnectedness of all library types for various goals, we include detail here for other types of librarians and library advocates to better understand school libraries and librarians and how they fit into the whole library ecosystem. When a public or academic librarian explains to a voter or legislator why school libraries matter and how they contribute to the strengths of all libraries, every library voice is strengthened; and speaking with *One Voice* in this way is essential to the success of the collaborative advocacy effort.

What Is a School Library?

The American Association of School Librarians (AASL) has written several position statements that define and clarify the role of the school library and the school librarian. AASL's position statement on an effective school library provides the following definition:

> An effective school library has a certified school librarian at the helm, provides personalized learning environments, and

offers equitable access to resources to ensure a well-rounded education for every student.

As a fundamental component of college, career, and community readiness, the effective school library:

1. is adequately staffed, including a state-certified school librarian who
   - is an instructional leader and teacher;
   - supports the development of digital learning, participatory learning, inquiry learning, technology literacies, and information literacy; and
   - supports, supplements, and elevates the literacy experience through guidance and motivational reading initiatives;
2. has up-to-date digital and print materials and technology, including the curation of openly licensed educational resources; and
3. provides regular professional development and collaboration between classroom teachers and school librarians.[2]

The Five Roles of the School Librarian

AASL defines five different roles of the school librarian: teacher, leader, instructional partner, information specialist, and program administrator. While these roles apply specifically to school librarians, we note that other types of librarians are also leaders, information specialists, and program administrators; their teaching and instructional partnerships look substantially different but still factor into their daily work at public and academic libraries.[3]

Teachers

As teachers, school librarians teach students how to find, evaluate, create, and communicate information. School librarians also teach students how to read for understanding, breadth, and pleasure and become enthusiastic readers. They teach students to be critical thinkers and ethical users of information. They teach students to understand and respect the diversity in our global society and be empathetic to others. School librarians also provide opportunities for students to collaborate for enhanced learning, to build on prior knowledge and construct new knowledge, and to reflect on their own learning.

Leaders

As leaders, school librarians work with the entire school community. The AASL's position statement on "The Strategic Leadership Role of School Librarians" states that school librarians

> provide effective leadership in areas of curriculum development, instructional design, technology integration, professional development, student advocacy, information literacy instruction, and collaboration. This is demonstrated by active involvement in and through school and district-level leadership teams, technology teams, strategic planning, literacy development, curriculum development, and initiatives that impact student achievement.[4]

The International Literacy Association also recognizes the role of school librarians as leaders of a school-wide culture of literacy. School librarians have an important role as advocates for literacy equity, as defenders of students' rights to read, and as providers of access. School librarians "promote, develop, and foster culturally relevant and responsive environments, as they curate collections that represent the ethnic and linguistic diversity of the student population." They provide all students with access to texts and digital materials that support their schoolwork, their personal interests, and their independent reading.[5]

Instructional Partners

School librarians collaborate with other educators in their schools, including classroom teachers, administrators, counselors, social workers, and psychologists, to positively impact teaching and learning. They co-develop, co-teach, and co-assess lessons with classroom teachers to meet academic standards and develop students' critical thinking, digital and information literacy skills, and cultural competencies.

Information Specialists

As information specialists, school librarians professionally curate and provide access to resources for their learning community. They provide expertise in emerging technologies, meaningful technology integration, and information literacy. They teach the ethical use of information and understand privacy, copyright, and fair use laws. They uphold the value of intellectual freedom.

Program Administrators

As program administrators, school librarians ensure that the mission, vision, and goals of the school library align with the educational goals of their school or district. They create and implement policies and procedures that ensure the school library is a safe space for all students and provides equitable access to resources for all students. They form partnerships with stakeholders and community organizations to expand the resources and services available to students. They advocate for their learners' access to robust school library collections and services.

The Impact of School Librarians

AASL's vision statement, "Every school librarian is a leader; every learner has a school librarian," calls for every student to have equity of access to a state-certified school librarian.[6] Multiple studies show that students with access to a school library staffed by a qualified school librarian have higher student achievement levels.[7] ALA's Committee on Library Advocacy has developed an infographic called "Students Reach Greater Heights with School Libraries."[8] (See figure 12.1 on the following page.) In its graphic form, the top step refers to higher education; the five stair

FIGURE 12.1 | **Students Reach Greater Heights with School Libraries (simplified for clarity)**

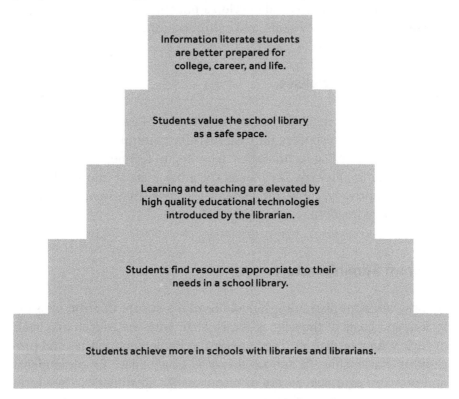

Information literate students
are better prepared for
college, career, and life.

Students value the school library
as a safe space.

Learning and teaching are elevated by
high quality educational technologies
introduced by the librarian.

Students find resources appropriate to their
needs in a school library.

Students achieve more in schools with libraries and librarians.

steps build from the basic premise that school libraries support students to achieve more, with the resulting proposal that these students will be more successful in higher ed situations if they've had the advantages offered by K-12 library resources and certified staff.

Each step in the infographic is further explained below and is supported by pertinent research:

- Information-literate students are better prepared for college, career, and life.
  - » Post-secondary institutions, employers, and civic life require the ability to find, evaluate, use, and create information in multiple formats.

» School librarians—schools' only certified information professionals—teach information, digital, and media literacies, as well as digital citizenship.

- Students value the school library as a safe space.
  » Students who feel safe and well-supported are more engaged in school and perform better academically.
  » School librarians provide judgment-free learning spaces, curate resources that nurture student health and well-being, and promote reading for pleasure.

- Learning and teaching are elevated by high-quality educational technologies introduced by the librarian.
  » Students learn to safely and constructively navigate tools and resources that deepen inquiry, collaboration, and creation.
  » Teachers enhance classroom teaching with resources provided by the school librarian.

- Students find resources appropriate to their needs in a school library.
  » School librarians curate diverse collections that support varied abilities and learning styles; and that provide mirrors, windows, and doors so that all students better understand themselves and the world around them.
  » School librarians empower students to embrace curiosity and learn independently.

- Students achieve more in schools with libraries and librarians.
  » Students with professionally staffed school libraries have higher reading, writing, and information literacy scores, as well as higher graduation rates.
  » Studies show that Title I students and English language learners achieve even greater academic gains with a certified school librarian.

Yet, other data shows that students currently do not have equitable access to school librarians. Investigations by Keith Curry Lance and Deborah E. Kachel have shown that inequities exist in access to full-time certified school librarians in terms of race and ethnicity. These inequities are "exacerbated for students living in extreme poverty, in more isolated locales, and in the smallest districts."[9] These inequities affect the ability of all students to be information-literate, and to be able to use the resources at their public and college libraries. The inequities thus impact the ability of all students to be prepared for college and career. They also impact the development of literate citizens in our communities. As stated in an opinion article, inequitable access to school librarians is "censorship of equal opportunity."[10]

Equity of access to school librarians is an educational equity issue which impacts all library types. It also impacts the development of literate citizens in our communities. Therefore, ecosystem advocacy for equity of access to school libraries staffed by state-certified school librarians is extremely important for the benefit of all students, all library types, and our democratic society.

Advocacy for School Libraries and School Librarians

State and local advocacy for school libraries is extremely important because most educational policy is defined and implemented at the local levels. Federal funding and guidance programs such as the Every Student Succeeds Act (ESSA) and the American Rescue Plan Act require state and local advocates to get involved to make sure school libraries are included in how the policies or the funding are applied in their state or locality.[11] Active participation in ecosystem initiatives by school librarians can help improve the strength of all libraries within the ecosystem. When the library ecosystem comes together to advocate for library core values such as education and access or intellectual freedom, the library voice is stronger, and the advocacy work benefits all library types. The "Comparison of Public, School, and Academic Libraries" (appendix C) offers a quick overview of how library types overlap to reinforce libraries' usefulness throughout life and illustrates the missions of each type that focus on the different needs of library users across time and life changes.[12] With this increased understanding across the spectrum of library workers, ecosystem participants can more easily work together towards advocacy goals.

School library advocates can work with other library groups (the state library, public library organization, academic library organization, and other regional library groups) that make up the library ecosystem to gather information and develop a shared agenda. (See appendix A, the "Ecosystem Agenda Building Templates.") These efforts should also include stakeholders such as students, parents, administrators, school boards, community members, Friends groups, and even civic associations and vendor groups. What are the important issues in your state around library funding, staffing, access, standards, resources, and so on? How can these issues be collaboratively prioritized? Once a collaborative ecosystem group with an advocacy agenda and priorities is established, the group can use this agenda and priorities to make an action plan for a legislative agenda and for building stakeholder and community awareness. The Ecosystem Continuum (see chapter 3), with its four pillars of leadership, communication, collaboration, and sustainability, can be used to frame the advocacy work and ensure its continuance.[13]

Building the relationships and process for communication across the library ecosystem is important to establish and maintain. As issues or legislation arise that may affect any part of the library ecosystem, these established relationships will speak in *One Voice* to address the issue or legislation. Vocabulary will be key: different libraries use the same words, but not always with the same definitions. One focus of the initiative will need to be the development of a mutual understanding of intents, goals, priorities, and the interrelationships between all ecosystem members. For example, just when considering ALA's Core Values of Librarianship, the word "access" has nuanced meanings across library types. All members of the ecosystem initiative should have the same understanding of the terminology being used and be able to share this meaning with external stakeholders.

The Education Ecosystem

The advocacy work of the ecosystem across all library types is important, but equally important for school library advocacy is the education ecosystem. When looking for organizations to collaborate on agenda-building, school library advocates can take a broad view of state organizations involved in the education ecosystem when considering whether to include outside groups of educators:

School Administrator Groups

- School board association
- Superintendents association
- Principals associations
- Supervision and curriculum associations

Education Associations

- Teachers union
- State reading or literacy association
- Subject teachers associations (such as teachers of English, science teachers, social studies teachers
- Counselors association

Parent and Community Groups

- Parent-teacher association
- State-level GLSEN or PFLAG organizations
- Race, cultural, or ethnic groups
- Other groups that support public education

Businesses

- Booksellers
- Publishers
- Chamber of Commerce
- Other businesses interested in a strong local K-12 system

School library advocates can also look at a broad spectrum of issues that may be important for school library advocacy. For instance, working with the state department of education to endorse standards for the school library, tighten school library guidelines, or partner on literacy efforts may be as important as working with the legislature on funding for school libraries or on legislation to support school libraries. These other organizations can also be important to help address adverse legislation that may arise.

Tips for School Library Advocacy

How might you begin to build your advocacy team for K-12 libraries working with the larger library ecosystem? Here are some basic tips to get you started.

Gather a Team

Establishing a library ecosystem group will enable you to build a team of advocates for library issues. Some school library issues resemble those for public and academic libraries; yet there are also some unique concerns in K-12 education that must be kept in mind. Ensuring that the ecosystem team understands the core issues, including the nuances that may not show in their own institutions, will be essential. Bringing together multiple perspectives and individual strengths will be key to addressing the problem, from identifying messaging to spreading the word.

Ongoing advocacy requires sustained effort and can be time-consuming. But a well-informed, organized team can help share the workload and keep advocacy efforts on track. Your state library or state school library organization may already have built a team that includes all library perspectives in your state or area. School librarians should try to understand the needs in public and academic libraries, just as they hope those same librarians will similarly understand the needs in school libraries.

Legislators often prefer to see all libraries together, rather than as separate constituents. When an ecosystem team builds a collaborative legislative "ask," it is easier for the elected officials to develop a coordinated response. Building legislators' understanding of the similarities across all libraries, as well as the specialized programs each offers the community, is as important as developing that same understanding across librarians themselves. Ecosystem thinking is not unlike IMLS funding. Can school library priorities be included in the overall library advocacy efforts?

Every school librarian should be doing advocacy every day by being the best they can be at their job—but all those individual librarians need the ecosystem team, which is a collaborative effort working in sync across all libraries to generate new ideas and energy for building advocacy.

Focus on the Benefits to Students and the Educational Community

School library advocacy should always be focused on the benefits to the students and the educational community, just as all library advocacy should be focused on the benefits to the patrons and community. Education stakeholders want to know how the school library and the school librarian improve student learning or support teachers, administrators, parents, and others within the school community. For instance, multiple studies have shown that student achievement is higher in schools where the school librarian:

- Instructs students, both with classroom teachers and independently
- Plans collaboratively with classroom teachers
- Provides professional development to teachers
- Meets regularly with the principal
- Serves on key school leadership committees
- Facilitates the use of technology by students and teachers
- Provides technology support to teachers
- Provides reading incentive programs[14]

Advocates should provide stories and data to stakeholders that support these impactful activities by school librarians. The library ecosystem group can put together key talking points for all advocates about school libraries and librarians and use a common language that centers students and the education community impact.

Educate Yourself about Legislative and Education Systems in Your State

It is important to understand the specifics of how your state legislature, local government, or state department of education works.

- How often does the legislature meet?
- What is the specific process for how bills are introduced and moved into law?

- What are the key committees, and who are the leaders in those committees?
- How can you find legislation, its text, and its status?
- How can advocates find information on their own legislators?
- What is the process for providing testimony on bills or entering positions (pro or con) on bills?
- Who are the key decision-makers in the state department of education?
- How does your state board of education work?
- How often does it meet?
- Who are its members?
- What influence do they have?

Experienced advocates within the library (or education) ecosystem can help educate new advocates about the legislative and education systems.

Stay Informed

It is important to be informed on state legislative and policy issues. There are tools available to help you track legislation. You can sign up for alerts or updates on bills of interest and committee meetings at your state legislature's website. You can also sign up for press releases or other informational newsletters from your state's department of education. Are there specific news outlets that report on educational issues that you can follow? The library ecosystem group can help to keep its members informed as legislation is introduced or updated. They can share relevant news articles and information on important policy issues.

Know Your Stakeholders

Take time to get to know officials, legislators, and your stakeholders—their background, their important issues, and the committees and boards on which they serve, as well as their voting record. Having this information is useful when you meet with stakeholders because it may help you find common ground with them, which may in turn help you connect your advocacy to the issues that are important to them. Legislators are important, but their staff is equally so: make friends with legislative staff. They typically have more time to meet with you and discuss issues, and they can help make sure that your information gets to the legislator. Aim to build consistent relationships with all stakeholders, including legislators. Having established relationships is important, so that when you want to influence decisions or legislation, you already have established communication channels and some common ground. By including a broad group of stakeholders in your legislative efforts, you are in fact building stronger public awareness of what your libraries are contributing to the public good. Public awareness is another face of advocacy, but one often passed over in the pressure to succeed in legislative efforts. Public awareness is how you inspire voters to elect supportive legislators, and to speak to current officials about library needs. It is important to have voices outside of the library ecosystem supporting your advocacy efforts.

There are different ways to get to know legislators, including attending their community events such as coffees or town halls, asking them to visit your library (perhaps for a special event or to read to students), writing them, or meeting with them in their office or virtually.

The library ecosystem group can work together to share information about stakeholders and legislators. It can also leverage relationships that ecosystem group members may already have with legislators.

Align Your Message to Each Stakeholder

In meetings, it is important to really listen to stakeholders. When you listen to stakeholders, you can find out more about them, and thus continue to build that relationship. You can find out more details about their priorities. This will allow you to adjust your message, if possible, to connect with them. It is important to remember that some individuals may have biases or points of view different than your own. In speaking with them, you are trying to inform and influence them, not win a debate. Having more than one person in a meeting with a stakeholder can be very useful. The participants can share different perspectives and help to keep a positive tone during the meeting. One person can be responsible for taking notes during the meeting and other participants can add details, as needed, later. Stakeholders will tend to have a set of priorities.

If possible, craft your message to connect to at least one of their priorities.

Provide Education or Information on the Issue

A large part of ongoing advocacy is educating stakeholders and legislators about school libraries and the role of school librarians. It is also important to educate stakeholders and legislators about your positions on legislation or policy. One-page information sheets can be useful to leave behind at meetings, to e-mail, or to distribute in other ways. A possible format for a one-page information sheet is to list the issue, recommend the solution, and then provide support information including any data, research, or stories. These one-page information sheets also help build a common set of talking points and language for all advocates to use. The library ecosystem can have a set of one-page information sheets based on the agenda and priorities that they have agreed upon.

Be Proactive

Once the advocacy priorities have been decided on, build an action plan and follow through with it. This may include contacting legislators and stakeholders on a regular basis, such as monthly, to provide them with information and news. The action plan may include scheduling meetings with legislators or stakeholders to build relationships with them. It may include a more targeted effort to reach out and get as many advocates as possible to contact legislators on a particular bill. Or it may include reaching out to offer testimony on a specific bill. Advocates should always thank legislators or stakeholders after meetings and provide them with any necessary follow-up information. Advocates should also be ready to respond to new issues or newly introduced legislation.

The Five P's of Advocacy

School library advocacy is an ongoing effort, and it is important for advocates to remember that sometimes change can take time. This is where

FIGURE 12.2 | **The Five P's of Advocacy**

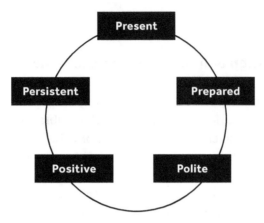

the "five P's of advocacy" come in: *be present, prepared, polite, positive, and persistent* (figure 12.2). Persistence is important in any advocacy effort. It is also important to be present. You cannot influence policy or legislation if you don't "show up" in order to make sure your voice is heard. In addition, it is best to be informed and knowledgeable and to be prepared for any meetings or interactions with stakeholders. In addition, being polite in meetings is also important. You cannot influence decision-makers if you are perceived as rude or disrespectful. Finally, it is important to stay positive—both in specific meetings about advocacy and in the long view of advocacy work.

An Essential Part of the Greater Whole

School libraries are an important part of the library ecosystem. While each library type may have its own unique mission and services, no library exists independent of the library ecosystem. School library advocates can work with advocates of other library types to help support advocacy efforts across all library types. Specific advocacy for school libraries is a necessary and ongoing effort strengthened by their participation in the library ecosystem, as well as in the broader K-20 education ecosystem which can help support school librarians in their advocacy work. See appendix A for additional resources.

NOTES

1. American Library Association, "ONE VOICE: Building a Strong Library Eco-system," www.ala.org/advocacy/ala-ecosystem-initiative.

2. American Association of School Librarians, "Definition of an Effective School Library Program," 2018, www.ala.org/sites/default/files/aasl/content/advocacy/statements/docs/AASL_Position_Statement_Effective_SLP_2018.pdf.

3. New York State Library, "Roles of the School Librarian: Empowering Student Learning and Success," Northeast Comprehensive Center (NY), www.nysl.nysed.gov/libdev/slssap/ncc-roles-exec-summ.pdf.

4. American Association of School Librarians, "The Strategic Leadership Role of School Librarians," 2018, www.ala.org/sites/default/files/aasl/content/advocacy/statements/docs/AASL_Position%20Statement_Strategic%20Leadership%20Role_2018-06-24.pdf.

5. International Literacy Association, "Literacy Leadership Brief: The Essential Leadership of School Librarians," 2022, www.literacyworldwide.org/docs/default-source/where-we-stand/the-essential-leadership-of-school-librarians.pdf.

6. Keith Curry Lance and Debra E. Kachel, "Why School Librarians Matter: What Years of Research Tell Us," Kappan, March 26, 2018, https://kappanonline.org/lance-kachel-school-librarians-matter-years-research/; American Association of School Librarians, "AASL Governing Documents: Vision," https://www.ala.org/aasl/about/govern#vision.

7. Lance and Kachel, "Why School Librarians Matter."

8. American Library Association, "Students Reach Greater Heights with School Librarians," infographic, ILoveLibraries, https://ilovelibraries.org/wp-content/uploads/2021/11/students-reach-greater-heights-with-school-librarians-7.pdf.

9. Keith Curry Lance, Debra E. Kachel, and Caitlin Gerrity, "The School Librarian Equity Gap: Inequities Associated with Race and Ethnicity Compounded by Poverty, Locale, and Enrollment," *Peabody Journal of Education* 98, no. 1 (2023): 85–99, doi: 10.1080/0161956X.2023.2160112

10. Lydia Kulina-Washburn, "Book Bans? My School Doesn't Even Have a Library: How Underfunding Is Its Own Form of Censorship," EducationWeek, July 26, 2022, www.edweek.org/policy-politics/opinion-book-bans-my-school-doesnt-even-have-a-library/2022/07.

11. Jen Habley, "AASL Conducts State Level Workshops on ESSA Implementation," *Knowledge Quest*, August 24, 2016, https://knowledgequest.aasl.org/aasl-conducts-state-level-workshops-essa-implementation/; Kathy Carroll, "How School Librarians Can Get a Piece of the ARPA Pie," *Knowledge Quest*, May 4, 2021, https://knowledgequest.aasl.org/how-school-librarians-can-get-a-piece-of-the-arpa-pie/.

12. American Library Association, "A Comparison of Public, School, and Academic Libraries: Vital to Our Communities," www.ala.org/sites/default/files/advocacy/content/Ecosystem%20Public%2C%20School%20and%20Academic%20Libraries%20Fact%20Sheet_0.pdf.

13. American Library Association, "One Voice: A Continuum for Stronger Library Ecosystems," www.ala.org/sites/default/files/advocacy/content/Library%20Ecosystem%20Continuum%20Updated.pdf.

14. Lance and Kachel, "Why School Librarians Matter."

13

PUBLIC LIBRARIES REACH EVERYONE

Jen Alvino Wood

ublic libraries today are brimming with activity. They are community centers with lively programming, a collection of resources in many formats on any topic imaginable, and a staff of librarians and library workers fighting for your privacy, First Amendment rights, and against censorship.

Public libraries bring to the ecosystem table a broad reach. They support everyone in their service area. People of all ages visit public libraries. Often the staff at public libraries collaborate with school libraries, have relationships and direct links to local government officials and legislators, and communicate frequently with large groups of community members. They are important connectors between all library types, opening the library adventure for some and expanding it for others. Tiny children start with storytime, graduate to K-12, and then return in adulthood as job-seekers, parents, or even just interested readers. Teens and adults may begin a personal research investigation in the public library and move on to university services as they gain confidence. University alums return to the public library throughout their adulthood. Taking advantage of these aspects of public libraries will truly benefit the larger ecosystem network; advocacy efforts of all library types are enhanced when they collaborate across the library ecosystem.

Librarians must work together and share with their communities the access that community members have, at any age, to all that libraries have to offer. All libraries, public, K-12 school, academic, and special, have in common many goals and core values. When these are shared across organizations, it enables collaboration and the coordination of efforts. Individuals pass through and utilize various libraries over time.

Public Libraries and the Sharing Economy

Public libraries were the origin of the sharing economy that often began with simple roots: community members sharing their resources with each other. From those early beginnings, libraries have changed over time to become vibrant community centers and free public spaces that support democracy and are open for reading and borrowing books and other materials, studying, and holding informal or formal public meetings.

The cornerstones of lifelong education and sharing among community members led to broad public support for public libraries. Libraries' missions across the public library sector are to provide their communities with information and ideas through resources and programming. These offerings can be anything from a children's storytime to a program about home organization. Libraries also provide space—space to simply sit in, to receive training in, or to provide a forum for community conversations.

Public Library Governance Structures

As more public libraries opened, a variety of governance structures came into existence. In states across the country, library standards assist governing bodies in the running of their libraries. The entirety of library services is usually overseen by a board of trustees. Public libraries have two types of boards of trustees, depending on the type of public library. Private nonprofit libraries have a governing board, and municipal libraries have an advisory board.

These boards of trustees are governing boards that hold the final authority for the libraries they serve.[1] Ultimately the board is responsible for the library and its resources, both fiduciary and legal, and is directly accountable to the public. Some duties may vary, but governing library boards typically oversee the hiring/firing of the library director, and delegate the day-to-day running of the library to said person. The board oversees the library and its staff, it fund-raises, it creates and manages the budget, sets policy, adopts the library's mission, vision, and values, and ensures the library's compliance with laws and bylaws.

Libraries that are municipal departments within the towns they serve typically have advisory boards. The members are appointed by the governing authority for the town, usually the town council.

The Voice of the Community

Most importantly, library boards tend to reflect the voice of the community.[2] Whether advising the director or overseeing the library more directly, library boards carry the voice and weight of the community's values and opinions and bring those with them to the work they do with the library. It's incredibly important for board members to be knowledgeable and to accept the Core Values of Librarianship in carrying out their duties.

Library Core Values

Most libraries adopt ALA's Library Bill of Rights and follow the core values of *access, equity, intellectual freedom, public good, and sustainability* (see chapter 2).[3] Sometimes these principles can conflict with community members' values and create friction. This friction can play out in a multitude of ways, from a complaint to the governing board or town manager to attempts to restrict access and funding.

This resistance can lead those community members to seek legislative action to make changes to how libraries function. Legislation that has come up in the past that affects public libraries has been centered around limiting municipal budgets through actions involving state and local taxes. Occasionally, other legislation has been aimed at privacy laws, obscenity statutes, and dissemination of information. More recently, however, the wave of legislation against libraries has not only been budget-based, though the attacks can certainly lead there. There have now been an increasing number of attacks on the very cornerstones of what libraries do and provide for their communities—access to information and freedom of expression.

Community members who disagree with some content that libraries provide may call for various legislative actions in pursuit of their goals: a rating system, committees to review collections or set new standards for new purchases, a system to categorize "objectionable" books or place them in inaccessible shelf locations, labeling systems that are biased, or even attempts to change definitions in state law so as to criminalize librarians. All of these legislative actions are ways to limit access to the resources that libraries provide, thereby attacking the fundamental principles of libraries and librarians.

Public library staff need to be informed, engaged, and participate in advocacy. We are experts in our field. We follow collection development guidelines and know the needs of our communities to help us choose the services and resources we provide. What we make accessible and provide to our communities should not be restricted based on one person's opinion or even a small group. The *Maine Library Trustee Handbook* puts it this way: "There is no place in our society for efforts to coerce the taste of others, to confine adults to the reading matter deemed suitable for adolescents, or to inhibit the efforts of writers to achieve artistic expression."[4] The library is open, accessible, and has resources for all. By advocating for the core principles noted earlier, library staff and supporters help ensure an understanding of the role of a public library in the community, increase support, and ultimately stabilize or increase funding.

Recent Legislative Advocacy Successes

Maine library advocates and voters have been successful in defeating legislation that would harm libraries in their state. Legislators have attacked library funding and content, and advocates have reacted quickly to push back and defeat the problematic legislation.

Attacks on Funding

Measures to limit, cap, or otherwise control the amount of taxes collected, or to limit both revenue and expenditures, have become more frequent. In Maine, we are grateful that it's been several years since we've had to fight such legislation. While these initiatives may lead to lower taxes, the results would be devastating to individual communities, as they rely on taxpayer dollars to fund services. Cuts to staff and services would need to be made if the following initiatives had passed:

- Property Tax Cap (Palesky Tax Cap)—In 2004, the Property Tax Cap proposed by Topsham community member Carol Palesky would have limited property taxes to 1 percent of a property's assessed value. This measure was defeated, but if passed it would have gutted municipal and school budgets and devastated local services, like libraries, that rely on either some or all their funding from the municipalities they serve.
- TABOR: the Maine Taxpayer Bill of Rights, or Question 1 (2006)—This measure was defeated on November 7, 2006, as an indirectly initiated state statute; these measures are citizen-initiated legislation that amend the state statute. If passed, the measure would have established revenue and expenditure limits for state and local governments, with specific limits for when those limits could be exceeded.[5] Similar to the tax cap, TABOR would have decimated funding for services like libraries.

Attacks on Intellectual Freedom and Librarians Doing Their Jobs

Legislative bills that restrict access to materials in any way impinge on intellectual freedom and the individual's freedom to read. In Maine and throughout the country, bills have been proposed that call for labeling systems, collection monitoring committees, and the filtering of computers and databases. These bills, if passed, would be detrimental to the collections and information provided by libraries. Librarians are highly trained professionals who curate collections for their communities. Limiting the ability of librarians to perform their job duties would restrict community access to information.

- Maine LD 94—Before the most recent wave of challenges in school and public libraries and proposed legislation regarding changes to obscenity laws, a local lawmaker proposed LD 94, An Act to Prohibit the Dissemination of Obscene Materials by Public Schools. This bill is very similar to ones proposed more recently in other states across the United States, and to Maine LD 123, which was proposed in early 2023. The LD 94 bill went through Maine's Committee on Criminal Justice and Public Safety and was voted "ought not to pass." The proposed bill would have eliminated the public-school exemption, which could lead to a teacher or administrator being charged with a Class C felony.[6]

When working to defeat these past cases, a variety of groups were involved. Fortunately, these efforts were resolved in favor of libraries. With the number of legislative actions in the past two years and their aggressive nature, a different strategy was adopted to fight and defeat detrimental legislation in Maine. Working with a library advocacy group, the Maine Library Association (MLA) and the Maine Association of School Libraries (MASL) began meeting to discuss adverse library legislation and how they could work together to defeat troublesome bills. They met with great success, as their group expanded to include several other organizations as part of their newly formed coalition—the Maine Humanities Council, Maine Writers & Publishers, ACLU of Maine, The Telling Room, the National Association of Social Workers Maine Chapter, and the Maine Council for English Language Arts all joined their advocacy efforts.

- Maine LD 123—If passed, this bill would have removed the educational purposes exception to the prohibition on the dissemination of obscene matter to minors. As mentioned above, LD 94 has a slightly different name, but ultimately both bills would have removed "public schools" as an institution exempt from the obscenity statute. This bill, rather than going through the Committee on Criminal Justice and Public Safety like LD 94, was proposed to the Committee on Education and Cultural Affairs. Just like LD 94, LD 123 removed the public-school exemption, leaving educators and librarians open to criminal charges. The coalition in Maine worked hard to successfully defeat this bill.
- LD 1008, An Act to Establish a Rating System for Books in School Libraries—This bill was copycat legislation similar to recently

proposed legislation in other states. Fortunately, this bill was also voted "ought not to pass." The bill required that publishers assign ratings to each book or materials distributed to schools. LD 1008 did not attract much public attention, but it had disturbing potential consequences for intellectual freedom.

From Coalition to Ecosystem

The Maine library ecosystem began at one of the Maine Library Association's summer retreats. A few board members formed a working group to learn more about ecosystem concepts and discuss ways the board could move these ideas forward to assist our advocacy efforts. Buoyed by the success of the coalition to defeat legislation in 2023, invitations were sent out, and a meeting was set up at the MLA's Annual Conference to discuss continued efforts to work together and explore the ecosystem further for future collaborations. The current work includes:

- *Building a legislative agenda*—Over the last two years, the Maine Library Association has expanded and strengthened its legislative advocacy by adding members to its Legislative Advocacy Group, offering training, and hosting a Library Legislative Day at the Maine State House. The group meets throughout the year to plan the annual advocacy day at the state capital and set the association's legislative agenda. The agenda will be helpful to the ecosystem partners to track upcoming advocacy opportunities.
- *Speaking with One Voice*—The Maine Ecosystem Coalition is beginning to form and take shape. The Maine Library Association is supporting ecosystem activities by convening quarterly meetings of all the partners. The group is creating a power map, setting goals and creating a strategic plan, and creating a contact list. The MLA created a discussion list and Google Drive to host documents for the group, and all members can contact one another as needed. It is imperative that the ecosystem partners continue to work together, communicate often, and set goals for the future of the ecosystem. Advocacy remains an important aspect of librarianship, and working together and speaking with *One Voice* will strengthen our messages.

Digital Public Library Ecosystem ————————————————————

The increasing impact of ecosystem ideas is evident in the fact that the word "ecosystem" is being used to describe collaborative work in libraries. ALA's "Digital Public Library Ecosystem 2023" report[7] was published in December 2023. Figure 13.1 shows a variant of the ecosystem we have been discussing, but an important variant.

Libraries sit at the nexus between ALA (and libraryland more broadly) and distributors of published materials, whether books or online resources—not to mention retailers and library users. The library ecosystem with ALA at the lead has been a key negotiator in efforts to find a

FIGURE 13.1 | **Digital public library ecosystem**

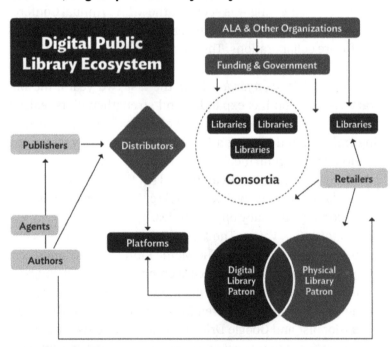

Source: Rachel Noorda and Kathi Inman Berens. "Digital Public Library Ecosystem 2023." December 2023. Work is licensed under a Creative Commons license (https://creativecommons .org/licenses/by/3.0/).

better pricing model for e-books and digital resources generally as purchased by libraries of any type, given that readers can often purchase e-books for substantially less than libraries can. Public libraries are leaders in this conversation, as they are the source of e-books for the highest percentage of readers; this is one of the nuances of their position in the comparison of library types.

Public Libraries Are Essential to Ecosystem Work

Public libraries are an essential component of an effective ecosystem. Public libraries can contribute to stronger messaging, improved impact, and broader reach when they are connected in partnership with other types of libraries and the whole range of library workers, supporters, and those who benefit from library services.[8] Like Maine, many states throughout the country are experiencing adverse legislation regarding libraries. In some cases, laws are being passed that are detrimental to libraries. Working together across library types—reaching across the gaps between our silos of habit—can bring broader awareness and stronger arguments against passing those laws that will have a negative impact on library services. We should take advantage of ecosystem thinking and build and strengthen our ecosystem to maximize its impact.

NOTES

1. Maine State Library, *Maine Library Trustee Handbook* (Maine State Library, 2021), www.maine.gov/msl/libs/admin/documents/Complete_Handbook_Mar4_ocr.pdf.
2. Maine State Library, Maine Library Trustee Handbook.
3. American Library Association, "Library Bill of Rights," www.ala.org/advocacy/intfreedom/librarybill.
4. Maine State Library, *Maine Library Trustee Handbook*, 184.
5. Maine Secretary of State, Division of Elections, "Maine Citizen's Guide to the Referendum Election, Tuesday, November 7, 2006,"
6. Rebecca Slocum, "Proposed Censorship Bill Voted Down in Maine," *Intellectual Freedom Blog*, February 25, 2019, www.oif.ala.org.

7. Rachel Noorda and Kathi Inman Berens, "Digital Public Library Ecosystem 2023," December 2023, www.ala.org/advocacy/sites/ala.org.advocacy/files/content/ebooks/Digital-PL-Ecosystem-Report%20%281%29.pdf.
8. American Library Association, "ONE VOICE: A Continuum for Strong Library Ecosystems," 2020, www.ala.org/sites/default/files/advocacy/content/Library%20Ecosystem%20Continuum%20Updated.pdf.

14

POTENTIAL PARTNERS IN LIBRARY ECOSYSTEMS

Sara Kelly Johns

The American Library Association is the largest organization supporting librarianship in its many aspects; it is a complex organization, often referred to as "Big ALA." Librarianship itself is a complex profession, much like the trees and forests in a biotic ecosystem. A tree has a solid trunk, from it grows branches, and from the branches sprout leaves or needles. The beauty of a tree is that the leaves are not all the same size and shape, and in many parts of the world the leaves change color with the seasons, enhancing the tree. The roots of a tree supply the nutrients (water and minerals) needed by the leaves for photosynthesis, which then provides the food for the tree. ALA's affiliates and groups, and the resources they supply, work together for a healthy, robust tree. Like forests, healthy library communities provide an ecosystem.

ALA Affiliate Organizations

ALA's affiliated organizations work as an ecosystem to ensure that all libraries and librarians have the professional connections needed to address their experience and focus. The people in these organizations reflect the world of librarianship as ALA members and can also reflect, support, and act in smaller, focused groups.

Former ALA President Dr. Barbara Stripling shared her reflections on the value of the affiliate organizations that are an integral part of ALA:

Affiliate groups provide the windows and mirrors in library eco-systems. They offer the opportunities for us to see ourselves more clearly because we are engaged in conversations and experiences with others like us in some way. We can see the huge diversity among those of us in the same affiliate group. But these groups also provide a lens (window) for others to see us and to appreciate the strengths that we share and the approaches we take to different situations. For example, PLA provides a window for me as a school librarian and educator to better understand the public librarian's role. BCALA [Black Caucus of the American Library Association] helps me understand the perspective and priorities of Black librarians.

Just as we all have multiple facets of our self-identities, so do we all have multiple connections to different affiliate groups. But that is the nature of ecosystems. They are flexible and change with the environment and current situation.[1]

Looking at the ALA's 2023 list of twenty-seven formal affiliates with an interest in libraries and librarianship or information science, we see broad and deep variety: organizations that reflect ethnicities, law librar-ies, research libraries, medical libraries, music, theater, and art libraries, even patent libraries—and more.[2] Each affiliate on the list appreciates the connection to others with the same focus, creating opportunities to solve similar problems—and they all have solutions and insights that will strengthen an ecosystem. The sections that follow are snapshots of a few of the many impactful affiliates that can amplify the *One Voice* of a li-brary ecosystem.

Association of Library and Information School Education

The Association of Library and Information School Education (ALISE) is the organization of faculty, staff, and students involved in education for the library and information science professions. ALISE was quick to step up to learn about ecosystem thinking and accepted an offer by the ALA ecosystem team to present a webinar on ecosystem principles to then teach library and iSchool students how to think in ecosystem ways.

These schools include courses on all types of librarianship, and the educators would benefit from knowing about *One Voice* efforts as they train their students to enter the library profession.

Association of Rural and Small Libraries

The Association of Rural and Small Libraries offers librarians in rural or isolated areas a network with colleagues in similarly remote locations who face the same challenges. Their advocacy work on behalf of small libraries includes a focus on collaboration and intellectual freedom, which may include advice on forming an ecosystem.

National Associations of Librarians of Color

In 2020, then-ALA President Julius C. Jefferson, Jr. issued a statement approved and supported by ALA's Executive Board: "ALA Takes Responsibility for Past Racism, Pledges a More Equitable Association."[3] In a post on the Association for Library Services to Children's blog that same day, Amalia E. Butler stated:

> As libraries work to become more intentional about improving internal and external relationships, reexamine outreach efforts, and reevaluate services provided to Black, Indigenous, and People of Color (BIPOC) communities, they can look to the work of NALCo for examples of best practices, positive outcomes, and leadership. BIPOC-identifying library staff and LIS students, as well as those providing library services within BIPOC communities, may also find opportunities to collaborate and participate.[4]

ALA affiliates that are part of the National Associations of Librarians of Color (NALCo) are:

- American Indian Library Association (AILA)
- Asian/Pacific American Librarians Association (APALA)
- The Black Caucus of the American Library Association (BCALA)

- Chinese American Library Association (CALA)
- REFORMA: The National Association to Promote Library and Information Services to Latinos and the Spanish-Speaking[5]

These affiliate groups joined together in 2015 to form a nonprofit organization, the Joint Council of Librarians of Color (JCLC), an ecosystem that advocates for and addresses the common needs of ALA's ethnic affiliates, giving them *One Voice,* a louder voice.[6]

Asian/Pacific American Librarians Association

One affiliate working as an ecosystem is the Asian/Pacific American Librarians Association, which was founded in 1980 to support the work of Asian and Pacific American librarians. Currently their membership is diverse, reflecting Asian, Pacific, and non-Asian heritages, varied identities and communities who appreciate the rich contributions to the profession made by the affiliate's members, such as the "Rubric to Evaluate Asian American and Pacific Islander American Youth Literature" (2021), which benefits all libraries.[7]

APALA, as a member of NALCo and the JCLC, connected with leaders of the American Indian Library Association to form a culturally responsive collaborative ecosystem. The duo advocated for the value of libraries and family literacy through the Talk Story program, which promotes the sharing of intergenerational experiences and cultural identities. The Talk Story program's mission statement states the shared values of the members of the two affiliates:

> Talk Story: Sharing Stories, Sharing Culture is a family literacy program that reaches out to Asian American and Pacific Islander (AAPI), and American Indian and Alaskan Native (AIAN) families and their intergenerational community members. Talk Story celebrates and affirms Asian, Pacific Islander, and American Indian intersectionalities through books, oral traditions, art, and more to provide interactive and enriching experiences. Talk Story grant funding supports library and community organization opportunities to highlight APIA and AIAN stories through

programs, services, and collection materials. Children and families can connect to rich cultural activities through Talk Story in their homes, libraries, and communities while challenging mainstream Anglocentric literacy practices.[8]

The affiliates' work creates opportunities for libraries to participate through grants and resources for libraries and community organizations, providing inspirational programming for communities that serve Asian, Pacific, American Indian, and Alaskan Native families.

Kindred Partners

Library-related national organizations, whether formal affiliates or not, can be strong potential partners when seeking stakeholders whose missions and work create paths not previously considered for success as an ecosystem. Consider the perspectives of the organizations below that may well be kindred groups.

Chief Officers of State Library Agencies

The Chief Officers of State Library Agencies (COSLA) brings together the top state library officials across the United States; they may be a state library agency's state librarian, director, commissioner, or executive secretary.[9] The organization enables them to discuss issues of common concern and national interest. COSLA members may also be personal members of ALA. Their agencies may or may not be organizational members of ALA, but they work together.

Council of State School Library Consultants

The Council of State School Library Consultants (CSSLC) is an AASL-related group of state consultants whose focus is to provide opportunities to network with, learn from, and support individuals in each state who work with school library professionals.[10] The council provides a national voice for effective school library programs and professionals and can make a difference in ecosystem networking. Both groups can extend ecosystem awareness and initiate collaborative action.

Library Consultants

Library consultants who come together for professional development and to stay up-to-date with best practices in librarianship are potential partners in ecosystem efforts. Library consultants are often members of ALA's Core: Leadership, Infrastructure, Futures division, the division for librarians and information providers who hold central roles in the areas of buildings and operations, leadership and management, metadata and collections, and technology.

The National Storytelling Network

The National Storytelling Network (NSN) cultivates a relationship with children's and youth librarians—but not all storytelling is for youth. The NSN's connections to communities, events, and education, and its commitment to diversity make it an organization to consider for an ecosystem that tells its stories widely and succinctly.

Expand Your Ecosystem, Amplify Your Voice

The groups and affiliates are clearly constituents of the library ecosystem and should be included in ecosystem efforts across the United States— and even beyond when these ideas carry over to other countries' library communities. There are many more library-related associations to include in support of ecosystem efforts. Those leading an ecosystem need to always be alert in search of groups, whether formal or informal ones. Since ecosystem teams come together as change agents to build community awareness and government support, the more voices included at the table, the better. And more voices, louder voices, get attention.

NOTES

1. Barbara K. Stripling, personal e-mail to author, September 30, 2023.
2. American Library Association, "Listing of Current Affiliates," www.ala.org/aboutala/affiliates/affiliates/current.
3. American Library Association, "ALA Takes Responsibility for Past Racism, Pledges a More Equitable Association," press release, June 2020, www.ala.org/news/press-releases/2020/06/ala-takes-responsibility-past-racism-pledges-more-equitable-association.
4. Amalia E. Butler, #alavirtual20 National Associations of Librarians of Color (NALCo), *ALSC Blog*, June 26, 2020, www.alsc.ala.org/blog/2020/06/alavirtual20-national-associations-of-librarians-of-color-nalco/.
5. American Indian Library Association, https://ailanet.org; Asian/Pacific American Librarians Association, www.apalaweb.org; Black Caucus of the American Library Association, www.bcala.org; Chinese American Librarians Association, https://cala-web.org; REFORMA: The National Association to Promote Library and Information Services to Latinos and the Spanish-Speaking, www.reforma.org.
6. Joint Council of Librarians of Color, www.jclcinc.org.
7. Amy K. Breslin, Sarah Park Dahlen, Kristen Kwisnek, and Becky Leathersich, "APALA Rubric to Evaluate Asian American and Pacific Islander Youth Literature," 2021, www.apalaweb.org/talkstorytogether/resources/apala-youth-literature-evaluation-rubric/.
8. Asian/Pacific Islander American Librarians Association, "Talk Story," www.apalaweb.org/talkstorytogether/about/.
9. Chief Officers of State Library Agencies, www.cosla.org.
10. Council of State School Library Consultants, https://sites.google.com/view/cosslc/home.

15

DIVERSE ADVOCATES CHAMPIONING LIBRARIES

Dorcas Hand

Non-librarians can be important—and even essential—contributors to an ecosystem effort. Journalists, literary agents, writers, publishers, library school educators, vendors and more. These are all groups who care that libraries remain essential contributors to their local communities, and so they are essential groups to invite to join any library ecosystem. Local parent-teacher groups, civic associations, and chambers of commerce might also make the list.

Building a Coalition to Include Non-Librarians

Anyone can be a library advocate. Any user of libraries may realize how important the library is to their community, or to communities in general. Each of these self-appointed advocates can speak out to increase awareness among other users that the library needs its funding renewed, its staffing increased, its hours adjusted to be more responsive to community needs.

Solo advocates often begin to speak up because they see a gap in public understanding or are concerned about an upcoming city council budget vote, for example. These enthusiastic individuals are not yet aware that they could bring other voices to the work. They are also unaware of the interactive ecosystem of libraries that could broaden their advocacy network further. And broadening their network has benefits beyond adding voices to their individual library of concern; they can discover how the library ecosystem speaks for all library types, and how the existence of all library types can strengthen the single library which drew their attention in the first place. Perhaps a savvy librarian will show the solo advocate how to find resources or skills from the state library agency or an ALA group.

That said, advocates are seldom very successful as single voices; a collective voice is stronger, and that strength can build on itself.

In previous chapters, we've shown how librarians of various types can join together to strengthen their efforts to raise awareness of libraries' needs and offerings to both the public and elected officials. Here, we discuss how non-librarians can join the effort. ALA offers opportunities for advocates who are not employed by libraries to learn from others who share their same enthusiasm. United for Libraries, a division of ALA, and Unite Against Book Bans, an ALA coalition/campaign, both offer robust websites with many resources available to support new advocates who are still finding their way. The members of both groups share an enthusiasm for strong libraries in their home communities and in the broader American society, though their paths to library advocacy differ.

United for Libraries

United for Libraries (often referred to as "United") is a division of ALA that has non-librarians as most of its members.[1] The tagline for United is the "Association for Library Trustees, Advocates, Friends, and Foundations." Its members also include any single person interested in advocating for libraries at any level, as well as corporate entities like vendors, publishers, and so on. United exemplifies and facilitates collaboration among like-minded individuals and groups from different library-related communities who may hold different perspectives and roles.

Trustees are those elected or appointed to the governing or advisory board of a library. *Advocates* speak on behalf of libraries locally or generally and on their own initiative. *Friends* may be members of an official Friends organization supporting a specific library, or they may be frequent volunteers at their local library. *Foundations* are incorporated organizations that can legally disburse money; these entities may be focused solely on one library, on many libraries, or on philanthropy more broadly, but they often like to remain aware of library issues. Corporate entities may be advocates of various types; they may support Friends groups at local or broader levels, or they may be broader think-tank or philanthropic institutions. Membership in United for Libraries can be the common thread that brings all these individuals and groups together.

United for Libraries illustrates how coming together to share information and collaborate on best practices for advocacy has strengthened the four types of voices—library trustees, advocates, friends, and foundations—that have joined forces into one organization. In turn, United implements by example the four pillars of an ecosystem: leadership, communication, collaboration, and sustainability. United has established useful communication channels among its members, providing a steady stream of ideas and best practices. Its conference programming at national and state events offers opportunities for collaboration with new audiences. United supports state organizations for trustees and library friends with access to resources and programming; the website offers a list of state friends and trustee groups to facilitate collaboration between them within a state and even across state lines when that may be useful. The Library Friends, Trustees, and Advocates Round Table (LiFTA) of the Texas Library Association is an example of a state opportunity for library advocates to share skills and ideas.[2]

United for Libraries encourages its members to advocate for *all* libraries in their communities; even if the United member is a trustee or friend of a public library, they learn that advocacy for local school libraries is also important because all libraries are interrelated. That said, United encourages more participation by school library advocates through its toolkit "Friends Groups: Critical Support for School Libraries."[3] The structure of school library governance differs from other library types because the school library is overseen by a school board that manages the entire school or school district; and not surprisingly, school board members are not directly focused on library needs in the same way that public library boards are. However, Friends groups are developing for school libraries, either by public school district or by individual schools. Campus parent groups—think PTA or PTO—often function as library friends groups for their school, raising funds for library materials or providing volunteer hours for projects. These school library support groups can benefit from United or LiFTA, once they realize the groups exist; they can also band together to build broader public awareness of the importance of both strong school libraries and the library ecosystem in general.

Advocacy Tools

An example of United's strong resources is the "Citizens-Save-Libraries Power Guide," which gives step-by-step actions for library advocacy.[4] Its web page provides examples of talking points, flyers, petitions, and more. An initiative to add student voices to United for Libraries, giving students impacted by community actions an opportunity to work together to have a louder voice, is only one of United's directions in the fight against censorship in libraries.

Public Awareness Tools

Additionally, United has developed with ALA a program called "The E's of Libraries" to promote public awareness of all that today's libraries, with the expert assistance of library professionals, help facilitate: "education, employment, entrepreneurship, empowerment, and engagement for everyone, everywhere."[5] The censorship movement denigrates the expertise of librarians as a way to undercut library policies and practices that welcome the whole of the community and its broad information interests. The movement even publicly disparages the graduate education that precedes an MLS or MLIS degree or other library certification. The phrase "E's of Libraries" offers a catchy way to remind advocates and their audiences of what professional librarians bring to the table—and that we need expert librarians in all of our libraries to protect equitable access to information for all.

Intellectual Freedom Tools

In the current climate where censorship efforts are growing, United has compiled a robust collection of tools to support advocates in intellectual freedom efforts.[6] These include resource guides, important definitions, and policy templates. With this audience of non-librarians in mind, the "Terms and Definitions Related to Intellectual Freedom & Censorship" is especially helpful to advocates beyond United members.[7] Anti-censorship conversations use many terms that can be misunderstood and are too often misused by supporters of censorship, making a source for clear explanations of these terms essential.

Examples of Collaborative Library Advocacy Efforts

While any single person can step up independently to advocate for libraries, library advocacy becomes much stronger when the *One Voice* joins a choir. There are a variety of choirs already in existence in various locations; we offer this list of examples. Readers will want to look in their own area for groups to which they can contribute their own personal efforts.

The Friends of South Carolina Libraries (FOSCL) is a statewide Friends group that not only brings together advocates from around the state and supports the formation and work of Friends groups, but also networks with neighboring statewide Friends groups like those in Tennessee, Georgia, and North Carolina.[8] "Share Your Story" is a FOSCL publication highlighting their 2019–2021 collaborative advocacy campaign.[9] Its forty-five pages drill down to the campus level to showcase libraries, with narrative and photos for each.

The Friends of Tennessee Libraries collaborates with the Tennessee Library Association and the Tennessee Association of School Librarians to form the Tennessee Library Ecosystem Consortium (TLEC).[10] Friends of Tennessee Libraries works with and supports other library organizations and library needs in their state. Their mission is to promote, support, and advocate funding for libraries on a local, state, and national level. They are a strong, supportive network of citizens promoting the value of libraries as institutions essential to democracy.

The New Hampshire Library Trustee Association offers strong training and networking activities.[11] Their website includes articles written in-house as well as outside links on topics such as First Amendment audits to ensure that library trustees from across this small state full of small and very independent towns will have useful information.

The Friends of the Saint Paul Public Library is a standout group nationally, supporting all types of libraries and library-related initiatives in the state and beyond. This group is also related to the Minnesota Association of Library Friends, thus amplifying the voices of members of both groups.[12]

The Friends of Libraries section of the New York Library Association (NYLA) offers meeting and award opportunities, as well as a strong trustee strand of programming at every annual state library conference.[13] NYLA's Friends of Libraries Section (FLS) membership represents various types of library-minded people, all working to increase the visibility of the value of libraries in the state.

The Cedar Rapids Library's Trustees Advocacy Committee in Iowa recently published a useful Advocacy Toolkit for their community.[14] This offers a strong example of how non-library supporters can contribute to library advocacy.

These examples demonstrate the range of organizations that have developed powerful ecosystems. We see independent statewide organizations of Friends and/or trustees. We also see local Friends groups, and sections of umbrella state library associations. Ecosystem ideas work in almost any context. Everyone has a place at the table.

United Against Book Bans

Unite Against Book Bans (UABB) is a separate campaign organized by the American Library Association to fight the "book bans [that] are on the rise in communities across the country."[15]

UABB offers a toolkit that supports any intellectual freedom fighter in the work of standing against censorship in coalition with like-minded library and First Amendment advocates.[16] This toolkit offers talking points and organizing tips that closely resemble the tools offered to librarians in their advocacy efforts, but it is specifically designed for non-librarians building their own coalitions, perhaps in concert with existing library organizations like United for Libraries. The Texas #FReadom Fighters, the Round Rock Black Parents Association, and the Texas Freedom to Read Project are examples of coalitions of people who are not employed by libraries but who have come together to adamantly oppose censorship in libraries.[17]

Unexpected Supporters Take a Stand for Libraries ⎯⎯⎯

Unexpected supporters abound. Valerie Koehler of the Blue Willow Book Shop in Houston, Texas, led a lawsuit to stop a 2023 state law attempting to require all book vendors to rate every book they might sell in the future or had sold in the past to a school; this is a strong statement of her commitment to library advocacy. Book vendors are only one example of "library advocates who are not librarians."

In December 2023, Penguin Random House filed a lawsuit against the Iowa Senate:

> This offers a second instance where entities outside libraries feel
> it important to stand for libraries and the Freedom to Read. PRH
> is a multinational corporation with an interest in state legislation
> because that law could impact sales well beyond Iowa.[18]

Other businesses have that same interest—or they should. The local chamber of commerce is busy encouraging new businesses to move to your area, and small businesses to open. These potential business owners want to move to a vibrant community with thriving libraries and schools to support the workforce and their families. Every community of advocates is different. There is no single road map to successful advocacy beyond the need to think outside the box. Every advocate, whether solo or part of a group, has the opportunity—the responsibility—to reach out to every individual with hope and the talking points tailored to them as best as possible.

Anyone Can Be a Library Advocate ⎯⎯⎯

Any user of libraries may realize how important the library is to their community, or to communities in general. Each of these self-appointed advocates can speak out in any of several ways. Having read this far, you are now aware that advocates are seldom very successful as single voices. Library advocacy becomes incredibly stronger when the one voice joins a choir. United for Libraries, United Against Book Bans, and a variety of other existing organizations can support your choir. The goal of a library ecosystem initiative is to train a chorus whose sopranos, altos, tenors, and basses are instead advocates of school, public, academic, and other libraries. Every advocate will want to use every available tool—including resources from established groups like United and UABB. The challenge now is to stretch your thinking, to develop new partnerships that cross organizations and library types, and all kinds of library supporters—all with the goal of stronger libraries for lifelong learning, for civic education and a strong democracy, for vibrant business communities. Spread the word. Take advantage of existing resources to establish a vibrant library ecosystem initiative in your community.

NOTES

1. United for Libraries, "What Is United for Libraries?" www.ala.org/united/about/organization.
2. LiFTA, "TXLA Library Friends, Trustees, and Advocates Round Table," Texas Library Association, https://txla.org/tla-groups/tla-round-tables/library-friends-trustees-advocates-round-table/about/.
3. United for Libraries, "Friends Groups: Critical Support for School Libraries," www.ala.org/sites/default/files/united/content/friends/school-friends.pdf.
4. United for Libraries, "Citizens-Save-Libraries Power Guide," www.ala.org/united/powerguide.
5. United for Libraries, "The E's of Libraries® & What's Your E?™" www.ala.org/united/advocacy/es-of-libraries.
6. United for Libraries, "Intellectual Freedom Resources for Trustees, Friends, & Foundations," www.ala.org/united/advocacy/challenges.
7. United for Libraries, "Terms and Definitions Related to Intellectual Freedom & Censorship," www.ala.org/sites/default/files/united/content/IF/if_censorship_terms_definitions_united_for_libraries.pdf.
8. Friends of South Carolina Libraries, https://foscl.org/home.html; Friends of Georgia Libraries, www.friendsofgeorgialibraries.com; Friends of North Carolina Public Libraries, https://foncpl.org.
9. Friends of South Carolina Libraries, ed., "Share Your Story," https://indd.adobe.com/view/60022646-750e-42a2-b4fd-1459d42d3404.
10. Friends of Tennessee Libraries, www.friendstnlibraries.org; Eryn Duffee, "Tennessee Library Ecosystem Consortium: Library Advocacy for All," October 2021, https://acrobat.adobe.com/link/review?uri=urn%3Aaaid%3Ascds%3AUS%3A0edbc679-fb8f-4d41-8d4e-b0801e42f1ea.
11. New Hampshire Library Trustees Association, www.nhlta.org.

12. Friends of the Saint Paul Public Library, https://thefriends.org; Minnesota Association of Library Friends, https://mnlibraryfriends.org.

13. New York Library Association, "Friends of Libraries Section," www.nyla.org/4DCGI/cms/review.html?Action=CMS_Document&DocID=144&.

14. Cedar Rapids Library Trustees Advocacy Committee, "Advocacy Toolkit," Cedar Rapids Public Library, 2023, www.crlibrary.org/advocacy.

15. Unite Against Book Bans, https://uniteagainstbookbans.org.

16. Unite Against Book Bans, "Toolkit," https://uniteagainstbookbans.org/toolkit/.

17. Texas #FReadom Fighters, www.txfreadomfighters.us/; Round Rock Black Parents Association, www.roundrockblackparents.org/our-work; Texas Freedom to Read Project, www.txftrp.org.

18. Jean Hessburg, "Penguin Random House and ISEA Partner in Litigation over SF 496," Iowa State Education Association, www.isea.org/about-isea/media-center/press-releases/penguin-random-house-and-isea-partner-litigation-over-sf-496; Penguin Random House, "Penguin Random House Files Lawsuit Against State of Iowa for Violating First and Fourteenth Amendments in Recently Enacted Legislation, Iowa Senate File 496," news release, www.penguinrandomhouse.com/articles/what-were-doing-legal-action/.

16

LIBRARY ECOSYSTEM LEADERSHIP AT THE STATE LEVEL

Dorcas Hand

Every state in the United States has a state library agency (SLA). These largely began as libraries for preserving state records, especially legislative records. As libraries came to be more common, the "generic" state library grew to include duties related to libraries across the state, thus "state library agencies." In some cases (e.g., Massachusetts), the state library remains assigned to state records while a separate state agency, the Massachusetts Board of Library Commissioners, works on behalf of all libraries in support of advocacy, funding, and best practices in librarianship. However, many state library agencies do both, like those in Virginia, Texas, Tennessee, and Washington.

In the twenty-first century, state library agencies may support libraries in a variety of ways, including managing and disbursing federal funds and developing and maintaining various library standards, whether related to facilities, staff certifications, or other state requirements.

Airplane View: Connecting and Convening

When we consider the library ecosystem from the airplane view, state library agencies are important for the connections they make between libraries across the state as well as across library types. These connections may take the form of professional development workshops; information retrieval consortia that often include database subscriptions or e-book access; the convening of task groups to develop or update certification requirements or collection development tools; and various other activities that support all libraries across the state. This role as connector or convenor is in addition to the essential role state libraries play in maintaining state and legislative archival and historical records, as well as, in a few cases, directly supporting the legislature for immediate access during a session and for archival access in the future.

State Libraries and Ecosystem Collaborations

In order to focus directly on advocacy, we did an informal survey asking state library agencies to tell us what they have been doing to implement ecosystem ideas. Seventeen states replied. Here are the highlights.

Funding Advocacy

Many state libraries work with other library organizations in their state to advocate for stronger state funding for all types of libraries. Since state library agencies (SLAs) are already disbursing federal and possibly other grant funds, the SLAs remain well aware of the budget situation for libraries across their states. While they are often constrained by law from any direct legislative advocacy, they can certainly support a stronger understanding of budgets, budget needs, and available grants.

Shared Database Subscriptions

Shared database subscriptions are a common collaboration which saves money. They also allow the research and price negotiations to be done centrally, thus ensuring that each library type is getting the best information products at the lowest cost to support their patrons' needs. This funding negotiation is a form of advocacy, as success requires that state legislators understand what the subscriptions include and how they are used to benefit the state's residents.

Union Catalog

Many states have a statewide union catalog to enable all library patrons across the state to search for titles held anywhere in the state. Once they find the required resource, the patron can perhaps request it through interlibrary loan or plan a trip to use it.

> Delaware created a statewide network and ILS. The original goal was for economy of scale savings, live data, convenience. But the power of a system is stronger than we expected—it's easier for public officials to fund a system! We received funding this FY (2022) to ensure school libraries can join too! First funding for school libraries here, ever.[1]

Interlibrary Loan

Interlibrary loans remain important. There will never be a time when every library holds every book or digital resource. Many state libraries facilitate the "back-end" systems that enable statewide interlibrary loan.

> The Wyoming State Library coordinates the statewide Integrated Library System as well as the interlibrary loan system used by all public and all community colleges. This allows for a single voice and coordinated messaging surrounding library infrastructure.[2] [We note that the "single voice" is strong but not inclusive of school libraries.]

Censorship

In the last few years, fighting censorship has become a very important concern and has been taken up by several state library agencies.

> The Massachusetts Board of Library Commissioners has been working with the Mass. Library System, the Mass. Library Association, and the Mass. School Library Association to support

library staff experiencing censorship attempts and challenges. "We have offered trainings for directors and trustees on collection development and intellectual freedom . . . We also organized and hosted recent Legal Issues for Libraries webinars . . . focused on library meeting spaces and library collections."[3]

The North Dakota State Library worked cohesively against censorship this year by encouraging individual testimony, both online and in-person each time a committee heard a bill to limit access to books. We worked alongside our state library organization (NDLA) to present a united front. We researched and offered statistics on the individual costs libraries would incur to review their entire collection for specific language the Legislature deemed harmful to children. We successfully saved our Online Library Resources from the scrutiny the Legislative body was advocating.[4]

Professional Development

The professional development offered by the state library agency is sometimes different from that offered by the state library association, but there are states where the SLA is the primary provider of professional development for librarians of all types. In some cases, the state library will support instruction on state systems, like database access, union catalog tools, and even consultants to support a regional system in strategic planning. Some states hold periodic meetings for library directors or offer discussion lists ("self-serve professional development") for different library interest groups. A few states, such as Arkansas and North Dakota, offer multi-day conferences. North Dakota's multi-day conference is called Stronger Libraries, Stronger Communities and welcomes all libraries to attend.

Summer Programs

Youth services benefit in many states from collaborative summer library programs, often organized by state libraries. Schools benefit indirectly from this effort as well.

Unusual Efforts

Now we will look at some more unusual efforts by state library agencies.

The Indiana State Library created an annual report that highlights the impacts of mostly public libraries in Indiana and provides this report to decision-makers in government, including state and federal legislatures.[5]

The Indiana State Library also collaborates with the Advocacy Committee of the Indiana Library Federation, a longtime umbrella organization which includes the Indiana Academic Library Association, the Association of Indiana School Library Educators, and many public libraries and public library trustees. The state library works with all these groups and institutional libraries (in prisons and hospitals) to provide training, databases, courier services, and LSTA mini-grants.

Nevada State Library and Archives has worked to restore the legislative appropriation for collection development to pre-pandemic levels.[6]

The Massachusetts Board of Library Commissioners works with the Massachusetts Library Association, the Massachusetts School Library Association, regional library advocacy organizations (for central and western Massachusetts), and their affiliates and partners to support strong funding for seven budget lines, most of which are interconnected to provide statewide access to library resources and services (statewide delivery, ILL, databases, e-books, etc.).[7]

- The Oklahoma Department of Libraries (ODL) is working to become a connector and convener of decision-makers, leaders, and ideas at the state level.[8] For example, the ODL is taking a lead in representing the interests of public libraries with the State Broadband Office (SBO). The ODL recently facilitated a direct connection with academic library leaders and the SBO to share information, improve understanding, build relationships, and grow coalitions. The ODL has worked with the state departments of Health, Human Services, and Education to help communicate and roll out new resources.

There has been a long-standing collaboration with the state's library and the various state library organizations—the Nebraska Library Association, the Nebraska School Librarians Association, the State Advisory Council on Libraries, regional library systems, and the Nebraska Center for the Book.

The Nebraska Library Association has a representative serving on the State Advisory Council on Libraries to participate in council meetings and report on association activities. Library Commission staff participate in association sections and committees. The Nebraska School Library Association (NSLA) has a representative on the State Advisory Council on Libraries and who participates in council meetings and reports on association activities. The council serves to provide information and advice to the Library Commission.[9]

The Arkansas Library Leadership Institute (ALL-In) program was created to develop leaders in the library profession and to strengthen professional relationships among all types of librarians in the state of Arkansas—both those with an MLS degree and those without.[10] ALL-In provides an opportunity for participants to learn and develop leadership skills that enhance the delivery of library services for all Arkansans. The Leadership Institute is held once every three years. A recent cohort included eighteen public librarians, six school librarians, four academic librarians, and two special librarians. Some states offer similar cross-type professional development through the state library association, like the Texas Library Association's TALL Texans Leadership Development Institute.

The Kentucky State Library met with representatives from the state university's library science school to foster a deeper relationship. This led to a webinar highlighting the state library's services, a presentation to a library class, and the writing of a letter of support for a grant opportunity. The state library also hosts meetings of the statewide Friends of Kentucky Libraries' board of directors.[11]

Libraries, in collaboration with the SLA, assumed the leadership role to create the Delaware Literacy Alliance across all sectors and ages.[12] The alliance's goals are to develop unified messages that build funding and capacity for senior and disability communities, including those currently deemed incapable of learning, and to reframe the message from a challenge to an opportunity.

It's a Start

When it comes to state library agencies implementing and supporting ecosystem thinking, there is much to be proud of, and still much work to be done. When libraries of all types collaborate to speak with *One Voice*, the issues they raise are better heard. *One Voice* for advocacy can bring greater awareness to patrons and voters and encourage them to raise their own voices in support of library improvements. It can also have greater impact in the legislative context, helping legislators understand everything that libraries do and how the library ecosystem needs their support. State library agencies can play an important role in the development of strong library ecosystems.

NOTES

1. Delaware Division of Libraries, https://lib.de.us/.
2. Wyoming State Library, https://library.wyo.gov.
3. James Lonergan, "Library Ecosystem Requesting a Bit More Information," e-mail message to author, July 10, 2023.
4. North Dakota State Library, www.library.nd.gov.
5. Jacob Speer, ed., "Indiana State Library and Indiana Public Libraries Annual Report," Indiana State Library, 2021, www.in.gov/library/files/2021Annual Report.pdf.
6. Nevada State Library, "Archives and Public Records," https://nsla.nv.gov/ home.
7. Massachusetts Board of Library Commissioners, "Affiliates," https://mblc .state.ma.us/about-us/affiliates.php; Lonergan, "Library Ecosystem."
8. Oklahoma Department of Libraries, https://oklahoma.gov/libraries.html.
9. Nebraska Library Commission, https://nlc.nebraska.gov/.
10. Arkansas State Library, www.library.arkansas.gov/.
11. Kentucky Department for Libraries and Archives, https://kdla.ky.gov/ Pages/index.aspx.
12. Delaware Literacy Alliance, "Delaware Literacy Alliance Strategic Planning Session," conference workshop, https://drive.google.com/file/d/1d3gk CXQz2Ww0Z6TTIvboNDY34WFdc5_J/view?usp=sharinh.

PART V
Ecosystems in Action

17

FIVE ECOSYSTEM JOURNEYS

Michelle Robertson

S ome ecosystems come together when facing a specific challenge; others are created as a part of their state library organization's infrastructure. This chapter will share stories from five state library organizations—New Jersey, Oklahoma, Tennessee, Utah, and Washington—that used the methods presented in this book to build a more robust library coalition in their states. Each state library association started its ecosystem journey in different ways. Some started because there was an immediate need to create an ecosystem to stop legislation that would have had a negative impact on all libraries in their state. Others began their ecosystem journey from an advocacy committee that already existed. Regardless of the origins of the work, all five of the participating state library organizations have established an ecosystem that is learning how to collaborate for the betterment of all library types in their state.

Utah's Library Ecosystem: We Are Stronger Together

Utah's library ecosystem came together when the chairperson of the Advocacy Committee of the Utah Educational Library Media Association (UELMA) saw the need to get librarians out of their silos in the face of impending intellectual freedom challenges. They invited the Utah Library

Association (ULA), the Utah State Library, Utah Library Media Supervisors, School Library PALS (a state education agency), the Utah Academic Library Consortium (UALC), the Utah Education Association, and other groups such as the NAACP, the Utah Pride Center, Equality Utah, the Utah LGBTQ+ Chamber of Commerce, and PIK2AR (Pacific Island Knowledge 2 Action Resources) to join the effort.

The Utah Library Association started their ecosystem journey by creating a space to facilitate coalition-building, communication, and action (when needed for rapid response) across organizational and jurisdictional boundaries. Then, they created specific tools to support their efforts. Once those tools were created, they shared legislative agenda items and talking points with members of their library organizations. They also developed and delivered coordinated talking points for committee testimony at the legislature and at Utah Board of Education hearings.

Utah's Ecosystem Journey

In 2021, when Utah Parents United began alleging "porn in libraries" through news outlets, the Utah Library Association leaders moved quickly to respond. The ULA reached out to a friendly state senator for advice about how to prepare for the legislative session, which began in January 2022. This legislator suggested the idea of a press conference as a way to change the framing and narrative. However, the librarians needed an excuse to call a press conference and to attract partners who were not librarians. They came up with the idea of writing and publishing an e-book that they could then share with legislators, parents, the press, and others. By dividing up the labor, they were able to write, edit, design, and publish the e-book in about a week. The ecosystem members agreed that the book didn't have to be great; it just had to be "not embarrassing." Together they published *Utah Libraries: Keystone of Healthy Democracy, Student Success, and Prosperous Communities*, a text in which the representatives of all library stakeholders spoke with *One Voice*.[1]

They used the e-book's publication to reach out to other community coalition partners, including the NAACP, Equality Utah, PIK2AR (Pacific Islander Group), and the LGBTQ+ Chamber of Commerce.[2] They invited these coalition partners to speak at a press conference in support of free access to information and against censorship." After the press conference, they "used their ULA collaborative space to draft and publish a number of statements in response to censorship. The ULA created an agenda that was shared with their ecosystem and beyond, demonstrating how their agenda-building tool could support an ecosystem as they learned to speak with *One Voice*.

Lessons Learned

The Utah library ecosystem's collaboration has effectively created a true cross-sector library community. All the partners collaborated to publish the e-book and to host press conferences, which built a strong sense of confidence. This confidence was reinforced by working together to develop a shared legislative agenda and the talking points, strategies, tactics, and tools used by the ecosystem. Frequent visits with legislators resulted in $750,000 for public libraries to spend on broadband infrastructure and the creation of a new "Library Specialist" position at the Utah State Board of Education. An additional valuable partnership has developed with the Utah Cultural Alliance, a well-respected, well-connected, and highly effective 501(c)(4) organization that advocates for the arts and culture.

Newly minted presidents in the ULA and UELMA are dedicated to continuing the advocacy work and strengthening the relationship with the UALC by bringing the chair of the UALC right into the ULA's Advocacy Committee. The group plans to establish a charter and to meet online quarterly. Private online communication tools continue to be used to facilitate ongoing conversations in both the "general" and "intellectual freedom" channels, and to facilitate the sharing of more "rapid response" or privileged, strategic information in their locked-down "steering team" channel. They have found that not spending much time on structure or hierarchy has worked very well. The ecosystem is egalitarian in spirit and practice.

Oklahoma's Ecosystem: Librarians and Community Members Working Together

Oklahoma's library ecosystem came to fruition when a past president of the Oklahoma Library Association (OLA), convinced the OLA's Executive Board that its Legislative Committee, as it was known at that time, needed a name change. Her reason for requesting the name change to "Advocacy Committee" was to help the members of the OLA understand that there are two kinds of advocacy: legislative advocacy, which typically includes advocating for or against any bill that is presented at the state or national level; and public awareness advocacy, which is advocacy for anything that makes your community aware of what you have to offer. OLA's Past President noted that "the term 'legislative' scares individuals and the word 'advocacy' was a more palatable term for OLA's membership, hence the need for the name change."[3]

The groups that the Oklahoma Library Association collaborates with include the Oklahoma State School Boards Association (OSSBA), the Motion Picture Association of America, the Oklahoma State Department of Education, the Oklahoma Workforce Innovation Board, and the Friends of Libraries in Oklahoma (FOLIO).

Oklahoma's Ecosystem Journey

Oklahoma's library ecosystem uses a group text that shares timely information with the ecosystem members. Online collaborative documents help create content that can be shared with members of the ecosystem. OLA created an advocacy calendar to remind their members that advocacy does not only happen in April, or at a point when legislators have created a bill containing issues that needed to be addressed by librarians. Talking points and a legislative agenda are also shared with the whole membership, so if a librarian wants to communicate with their legislator, they know the key topics that need to be covered.

The OLA's ecosystem writes reactive op-ed pieces in response to news stories or other problematic op-eds.[4] They have a lobbying group that helps guide them on legislative issues and provides media training for those who speak to the press.

Lessons Learned

The Oklahoma ecosystem benefits from collaboration because it builds confidence among the active members of the ecosystem. Learning to work with community members in creating a robust ecosystem has served the OLA well at times when legislative issues need to be dealt with at the local, state, or national level. Based on the ecosystem's experiences with various bills that were brought to the attention of their advocates, there are times to be either proactive or reactive to a situation, and then there are times when it serves the ecosystem to be quiet but ever watchful of what is going on in their communities.

Washington's Ecosystem: Collaboration and Communication Are Key

Until recently, the Washington Library Association (WLA) and the Washington Library Media Association (WLMA) were two separate groups; but the WLMA has now become the School Library Division of the WLA. Now that they are together, they are stronger advocates to stand for education in the state of Washington. The Washington library ecosystem also includes the University of Washington's Center for an Informed Public. The need to methodically advocate for school librarians required that the librarians build their ecosystem community quickly to work against entrenched legislative attitudes. The time spent bridge-building mattered to the impact of the legislative effort. (See chapter 9 for a full discussion of that work.)

Washington's Ecosystem Journey

The WLA's leadership has built communication channels that keep its membership focused on advocacy efforts and involved in the work both locally and statewide, including an online collaborative document and group text messaging to encourage easy communication as they prepare for legislative sessions and other issues that pop up in various communities. See the text box on the following page for a blog post published by the WLA ecosystem. WLA prepared the following collaborative messaging:

We believe all Washington students deserve access to strong school library programs directed by qualified Teacher Librarians. Decades of research confirm that students with strong school library programs and qualified Teacher Librarians have better educational outcomes and are more prepared for postsecondary education. This is especially true for students who experience poverty or other risk factors. However, school library programs in Washington are currently not equitably distributed, with those most in need of strong school libraries having the least access to them. We hope you use this website (https://sites.google.com/view/k12libraries4allwa/home?pli=1) to learn about the importance of all school libraries for Washington students. We are committed to working toward equity in school library staffing for Washington's students.

_____

Source: Eryn Duffee and Sarah Logan, "K12Librarians4AllWA Campaign," www.wla.org.

Lessons Learned

Committee members in the WLA attend other committee meetings on a regular basis, for example, the Advocacy chair attends the School Library Division board meetings so communication can easily flow between those two committees. The WLA found that creating a decision tree in their communication policy helps them create statements quickly when legislative issues arise. The decision tree also provides support to all library types at a point in time when they are having to deal with a significant issue. The WLA also found a way to create continuity when the leadership role rotates to a new person every year.

New Jersey's Ecosystem: Speaking with One Voice Makes Us Stronger

The New Jersey Association of School Librarians (NJASL) saw the need for advocacy when a 2016 survey to understand the status of school libraries across New Jersey indicated the need to pass legislation to preserve school librarian positions.[5] The NJASL partnered with the New Jersey Library Association (NJLA) to establish a joint advocacy coalition that led to the hiring of external consultants for advocacy training. The group's goal was to hone their advocacy skills in order to get two bills passed in the state legislature: an information literacy bill and a school librarian/ student ratio bill. New Jersey librarians activated a broad ecosystem that included the NJLA, the NJASL, the New Jersey Education Association (NJEA), the New Jersey Principals and Supervisors Association, New Jersey School Boards Association, New Jersey Association of School Administrators, Garden State Coalition of Schools, Save Our Schools NJ, New Jersey Association of School Nurses, and Computer Science for All (CS4NJ), as well as a team of unaffiliated advocates which included retirees, academic librarians, and actively working school librarians who were able to offer presentations, create infographics and op-ed articles, and work on opportunities to network with stakeholders across the state.

New Jersey's Ecosystem Journey

The New Jersey ecosystem's adventure began when the legislature's structure and process proved challenging for the NJASL: the library bills repeatedly had sponsors but could not get out of committee. Each year, the advocacy coalition would have to start from the beginning with new sponsors and new bill numbers. By building relationships with key contacts, many voices were ready to speak to legislators right up to the final moments of the vote.

The NJASL ecosystem effort was continuous. They were always brainstorming, building relationships with stakeholders, and looking for various avenues to make progress with legislation.[6] The outside consultants, as well as the NJEA, were instrumental in the coalition's eventual success. Between September 2020 and the spring of 2021 (six months), online petitions to save school librarian positions raised the legislature's awareness. Meetings with legislators, the president and vice president of the State Board of Education, New Jersey Department of Education staff members, and the head of Save our Schools NJ were also impactful. In the summer of 2021, they held two town hall-style meetings with legislators, with positive results.

When New Jersey's school library association started to create their ecosystem, they chose to communicate via e-mail, text messages, and online collaborative documents. By using all of the communication tools available to them in strategic ways, they increased their effectiveness.

Lessons Learned

With the help of their advocacy consultants, the New Jersey ecosystem was able to create targeted social media advertising and utilize the Save School Librarians platform to create petitions to try to save library positions, as well as to create messaging so that members could easily contact their legislators to ask them to co-sponsor the bills.

Tennessee's Ecosystem: Fight against Book Banning

In late 2020, the Tennessee legislature began working on some problematic bills related to intellectual freedom. The Tennessee Library Association (TNLA) and the Tennessee Association of School Librarians (TASL) saw an immediate need to collaborate. The Tennessee Library Ecosystem Coalition (TLEC) was formed from this collaboration. They also worked with the Friends of Tennessee Libraries (FOTL).

Tennessee's Ecosystem Journey

The Tennessee Library Association ecosystem had to find a way to deal with an inflammatory newspaper article published by a local school board member in the *Chattanooga Times Free Press*. When TLEC learned of the article, they collaborated to write a joint position statement, which they e-mailed to the local school district's school board members and superintendents.[7] The same position statement was also submitted and published in the *Tennessean* newspaper and picked up by ALA. TNLA's ecosystem came under attack by the Moms for Liberty and mobilized a message to respond. TLEC became an internal bridge to link several separate library organizations that worked together to fight problematic legislation and local policies. Once the crisis was averted, TLEC formalized some processes for sustainability to face the continuing onslaught of legislative issues.

Lessons Learned

Tennessee's ecosystem came together almost overnight, as it seemed to outsiders. They collaborated to speak with *One Voice*. They learned that their voice was more assertive when they shared the same message.

What's Next?

New Jersey, Oklahoma, Tennessee, Utah, and Washington are just a few of the states that have created ecosystems in order to advocate with *One Voice*. While each of the five states started their journey differently, they all used leadership communication, collaboration, and sustainability as they learned to work together for the betterment of libraries in their state. Start your journey today. Find like-minded individuals and start to create your own library ecosystem.

Acknowledgments

I would like to thank the five state library associations that contributed to this chapter. For sharing their stories in how their ecosystems were created and how they work their way through issues as they have occurred in their communities. Taking the time to share their stories with us will help others successfully create their ecosystems.

NOTES

1. *Utah Libraries: Keystones of Healthy Democracy, Student Success, and Prosperous Communities* (Utah Library Advocates, 2021), https://ula.org/guide/.
2. Rita Christensen, "ULA Joins Press Conference," Utah Library Association, press release, December 15, 2021, https://ula.org/content/2021/12/ula-joins -press-conference/.

3. Lisa Wells, Ecosystem Interview with Michelle Robertson, August 2023.

4. Cherity Pennington, "Viewpoint: Students Best Served, Freedom Protected when Librarians, Parents Are on Same Page," *The Oklahoman*, February 20, 2022, www.oklahoman.com/story/opinion/2022/02/20/viewpoint-book -censorship-oklahoma-elsewhere-endangers-freedom/6796756001.

5. Maureen Donohue and James Keehbler, "School Library Programs in New Jersey: Building Blocks for Realizing Student Potential with ESSA Legisla- tion Opportunities," New Jersey Association of School Librarians and New Jersey Library Association, April 2016, https://njasl.org/resources/ Documents/2016ESSAandNJSchoolLibraryPrograms.pdf.

6. Carly Sitrin, "Lawmakers, School Librarians Say Now Is the Time to Teach Information Literacy," *Politico*, February 23, 2021, www.politico.com/states/ new-jersey/story/2021/02/23/lawmakers-school-librarians-say-now-is-the -time-to-teach-information-literacy-9425555.

7. The joint statement can be found on TNLA's website: "Joint Statement on HB0800/SB1216 from Tennessee Association of School Librarians, Tennes- see Library," Tennessee Library Association, news release, March 29, 2021, www.tnla.org/news/581641/Joint-Statement-on-HB0800SB1216-from -Tennessee-Association-of-School-Librarians-Tennessee-Library-.htm.

18

THE MYTH OF GOING IT ALONE

Megan Cusick

L ibrary professionals are a strong and resourceful bunch. Whether a library has a large staff or just a department of one, daily decision-making and tasks are often left to one individual. Our professional training prepares us to meet various responsibilities and challenges involved in the curation of resources, program planning and implementation, management of the physical space, and direct service to patrons. And so, it is no surprise that librarians are a self-sufficient bunch.

Yet, librarianship is also a social enterprise premised on advancing the collective good. It requires the thoughtful stewardship of public and/or private funds to fulfill that enterprise. A wide range of stakeholders—both library users and non-users—need to recognize the impact of the various libraries in their sphere in order for those libraries to enjoy the backing of the communities they serve, as well as their continuing financial and policy support. Achieving this is the ongoing work in which every library professional engages, consciously or not, and which is foundational to all advocacy, as well as to the health of the library ecosystem.

Comparing Ecosystems

None of us goes at it alone in librarianship. Attempts to operate outside the ecosystem, even in the most capable hands, eventually become unsustainable. At first glance, a healthy library ecosystem seems unaware of itself. Individual librarians, libraries, or systems may seem to churn along effectively without a network of support. Take a closer look, however, and there are significant connections that undergird the effectiveness of each unit individually and the ecosystem as a whole. In a forest, these interconnections exist through a dense mycorrhizal underground network of tiny fungal threads that are interlaced with the trees' roots. Our understanding of its sophistication and reach of this "mycorrhizal network" continues to unfold. What we do know is this complex underground system of fungal threads allows individual trees to share access and transfer water and nutrients with other trees of the same species, thus safeguarding the sustenance of their species as a whole. A tree that holds its roots tightly at its base may appear, above ground, to be functioning like the trees around it. But that is a short-term proposition. Eventually, the tree will be unable to take in or retain sufficient amounts of water and essential nutrients and will lack adequate defense for itself, let alone any ability to support other trees or plant life against an unexpected threat or attack.

A Chinese proverb instructs that the best time to plant a tree is twenty years ago; the second-best time is now. While building a healthy ecosystem takes time, this adage emphasizes that the time to take action is now. A tree planted today may not offer any shade for some years, but it will be on a course to do so far sooner than the tree that is scheduled for future planting. And its other contributions to the ecosystem—from sharing nutrients to improving the soil chemistry to cleaning the air—commence upon planting.

Just as a healthy ecosystem is the primary source of strength for a sustainable forest, the same goes for libraries. A healthy library ecosystem enables an individual library to sustainably carry out its mission, respond to the needs and aspirations of its community, and support individual library professionals, institutions, associations, and related organizations. A healthy ecosystem aligns with and facilitates the advocacy work of library professionals that is needed to generate ongoing support *for* all libraries and *from* all constituencies, whether the community, administrators, funders, or policymakers.

Strength in Numbers

A school librarian who is actively engaged with their library and education associations, with parent organizations, or with neighboring public and academic libraries is far better positioned to advance a priority or respond to a threat than an equally skilled librarian who has not nurtured those connections.

Similarly, a public librarian who is connected to their board and Friends group, to the local chamber of commerce, to community and civic institutions, and to neighboring school and academic libraries will be better positioned to get others to take action not just in a crisis, but for the ongoing work—for example, board elections, policy changes, or budget passage—that helps prevent or minimize crises. In both cases, a chorus of supportive voices, a robust organizing capacity, and connections to decision-makers have already been established, making rapid mobilization a more viable endeavor.

Conversely, if that foundational work has not been done and a crisis arises, the toll on individuals and communities can be profound and lasting. If community members, board and Friends group members, fellow faculty, parents, and allied organizations are not able to speak to the library's work and its benefits to the community, then sharing that necessary background, identifying supporters, and securing commitments to action takes valuable time away from the actual advocacy work itself. In some situations, librarians or board members in the crosshairs are unable to speak publicly on an issue, necessitating that others in the ecosystem be prepared to advocate on our behalf. Lisa Varga, executive director of the Virginia Library Association, had this message in her "Hammer, Vise, Lever" presentation at the 2023 LibLearnX conference:

> It can be really challenging, really isolating, when a crisis comes to your library or your community. Building relationships within and beyond the profession—before a crisis occurs—allows us to show up for each other, to speak up when others cannot, and to employ the best tools for a particular situation and at a particular moment.

Crises can place an incredible strain on all parties involved, particularly those who are required to do emergency outreach and organizing work above and beyond their regular professional responsibilities—and possibly entirely outside of the workplace, adding stress to their family and personal life. Burnout and emotional strain are very real concerns.

Consider the library ecosystem in which you currently operate and where you need to build additional intentionality into ensuring the health of that system. Expand from there. Prioritize and plan and, whenever possible, don't wait for a crisis. While you will probably be able to overcome the crisis, the strain it will place on the ecosystem and its individual units—most importantly, the people impacted—can have lasting detrimental effects on the entire ecosystem, particularly when a crisis catches you unprepared.

Reaching across the Profession

As a profession, we must recognize the mutuality of our work and the interconnectedness of our communities that engage with libraries at different stages of life, in different locations, and for different needs. Just like the trees in a forest, if we hold our own roots tightly only for the purpose of sustaining ourselves, we weaken both ourselves and the larger library community. Extending those roots is central to developing a web of mutuality. And those roots must be nurtured continuously, not just when there's an urgent need.

This includes integration across library types. The users' impressions of *all* libraries are usually informed by their experiences at *one* library. Similarly, the community's perception of a library's value should be broadened by its members' exposure to that library as part of the larger ideal. A student without access to a school library is likely to be ill-prepared for post-secondary research in an academic library, or for regular engagement with their local public library as an adult. The taxpayer who doesn't understand the transformational value of the public library to their entire community (users and non-users alike) is less likely to become what the OCLC and ALA's joint study, *From Funding to Awareness,* described as a "super supporter."[1]

Moreover, the trends impacting one type of library are likely to impact other types of libraries, too. From censorship to budget cuts, if it happens in one place, it is likely to happen in another. Conversely, when all librarians can speak with authority about the importance of each element in the library ecosystem, all parts of the ecosystem benefit. For example, academic librarians who show up to speak on behalf of maintaining professionally staffed high-school libraries—as they have done in localities across the country—are advocating for the health of all libraries, and for the communities they serve. Similarly, the school librarian who speaks to their county commissioners about funding for the public library's teen space is advocating for all libraries, for the youth in the community, and for the vibrancy of the community overall.

It is important, therefore, that *all* types of libraries, their staffs, their boards, and their professional associations regard each other as pieces of a whole rather than as competitors. Budgets notwithstanding, librarianship is not a zero-sum game. While the distinctions between library types are crystal clear within the profession, most decision-makers and members of the public hear the word "library" without a distinguishing prefix. If we are not unified in our messaging or, even worse, if we undermine the messaging of our colleagues, all our advocacy efforts are jeopardized.

Library associations, whether unified or separate, have an important role to play in facilitating the library ecosystem, in helping to align its priorities and unify its messaging. The engagement must be multidirectional and ongoing. This is particularly crucial in legislative advocacy, where disjointed agendas may confuse the very decision-makers upon whom libraries rely for support.

Toolkits

In addition to the resources available through the Ecosystem Toolkit, ALA offers a "State Legislative Toolkit" and an "Advocacy Action Plan Workbook," which can assist with planning around a specific issue or campaign. See appendix D for more information.

Extending Roots beyond Libraries ──────────

While engagement with the full range of library types and organizations is key to an ecosystem's survival and sustainability, connections beyond libraries with the broader community are also essential to it. Each local and state ecosystem is unique due to the libraries, the geographic setting, the population served, current trends, and the professional and volunteer staff. These factors also present opportunities for each unit of the ecosystem to enhance the whole through *collaboration*, *partnerships*, and *coalitions*. First, let's define what each of these represents.

Collaboration

Collaboration is the act of working together, and, in the context of librarianship, it is the air we breathe. Formal and informal models of collaboration are plentiful, in libraries of all types. School and academic librarians collaborate with faculty, administrators, and researchers. Public librarians collaborate with other municipal or county departments. State library agencies collaborate with libraries across the state, as well as with other state agencies, to maximize their resource-sharing and reach.

Partnerships

Partnerships usually involve a formal agreement between two or more organizations to combine resources towards a specific end. Again, library examples abound and often involve the complementary expertise and resources of the library and external organizations. A local public library, for example, may partner with the regional workforce development office and state or local officials to provide articulated support for jobseekers.

Coalitions

Coalitions are groups that agree to pursue a specific goal together. That goal is often laser-focused, for example, the passage of a particular piece of legislation or action on a specific issue in which each of the member groups has a vested stake. Sometimes the coalition will be led by the library community, and sometimes the coalition will be led by another organization. What makes a strong coalition? First, alignment around a specific goal. Second, clear delineation of responsibilities and tasks towards achieving that goal. And third, communication. Ongoing communication ensures that all members of the coalition maintain a clear understanding of their role in making decisions, taking action, and engaging with the coalition.

Tip Sheet: Building Successful Coalitions

Coalitions can be a powerful force in advancing legislative or advocacy goals, and bringing different strengths, areas of expertise, and stakeholders together for greater impact. It is important to enter into coalition work with a clear idea of expected outcomes and how the coalition can better move your organization towards those outcomes. Here are some tips to forming a successful coalition:

- Articulate the goal(s) of the coalition.
- Identify who will lead the coalition; this can be a single organization or multiple organizations.
- Determine what resources are needed for the coalition's work, what the lead organization(s) will commit, and what participating organizations will commit.
- Clearly outline decision-making processes that emphasize consensus-building.
- Invite potential coalition members to join. Ensure that the coalition represents diverse and trusted voices who bring relevant expertise, are connected to the community and/or decision-makers, and who are committed to the coalition's goals.
- Develop a time frame for the coalition's work and an action plan with clear objectives and responsibilities.
- Announce the coalition and, if desired, invite other organizations to join.
- Establish regular communications via meetings and updates.
- Maximize the power of collaboration by tapping into the unique strengths of various coalition members.

- Monitor the coalition's progress and adjust the action plan as needed.
- When success is achieved, evaluate whether the coalition should continue towards a related goal or disband.
- Throughout the work, recognize the contributions of coalition members and celebrate their achievements.

There are some instances where an organization can be most effective by participating in coalitions led by others, particularly when the issue is not in the organization's primary portfolio. Similar considerations should guide the decisions about joining a coalition.

The American Library Association, through its Public Policy and Advocacy Office, is active in several coalitions in the interest of advancing national policy and legislation that supports libraries, library workers, and the communities served by libraries. Some of these coalitions are focused on education, others on broadband and digital equity, workforce development, or copyright. As the national voice for libraries and library workers, ALA contributes recognized expertise, trusted stewardship, and the field experience of members in cooperation with other organizations to bolster the work of these coalitions.

One example of a library-led coalition is the Unite Against Book Bans campaign,[2] launched by ALA to combat coordinated efforts to restrict access to reading materials through local book challenges, as well as through policy and legislative efforts. Some of the coalition members are already closely connected to ALA through existing collaborations and partnerships. Other coalition members are not formally connected to the association but intersect with the association's work in the key area of protecting intellectual freedom and the rights of individuals to access information.

How do you identify the best groups for collaboration, partnership, and coalition? In librarianship, we always start with those core values that undergird our work. Then, look at the mission of your institution along with its strategic priorities, which should point you in the direction of operationalizing those core values. Consider the networks you already have and where there may be opportunities to deepen or extend them, and where new connections can be made. Also consider where you have opportunities to build relationships over time. A collaboration with a

FIGURE 18.1 | **ALA's Core Values with coalition partners and intersecting interests**

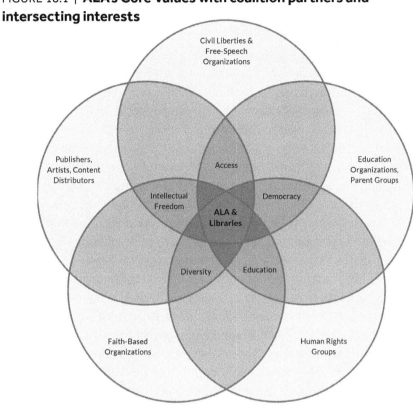

Source: Megan Cusick

new group on a specific project may lead to deeper work together in the future. Focus on the intersecting values of your library or organization with the values and priorities of other organizations in your community or in your state (figure 18.1).

Implementing the Agenda

Equally important is being clear on what you need to achieve and what is needed to get you there. Very little in the advocacy realm is "one and done." Legislative advocacy is a good example of how it may take several years to see progress on a particular issue. Advocates must build support, educate lawmakers and influencers (e.g., the press, and possibly the business/civic/education community), identify champions, and then press for passage of a particular bill. This can be arduous work, and each step of the process comes with its own land mines as well as opportunities. Moreover, advocacy is often iterative, building upon the efforts that came before and the learning taken from that work. Distributing that work across the ecosystem allows you to tap into the different expertise, connections, resources, and audiences of an enhanced network.

Just as a diverse biological ecosystem is stronger than a monoculture, a variety of perspectives, experiences, and strengths will elevate the work you undertake and fortify the fabric of your extended network. Consider a broad range of organizations as you extend your roots. Education, cultural, and civic organizations easily spring to mind. Also consider the business community, labor unions, arts organizations, the legal community, civil and human rights groups, content creators, and faith-based and interfaith organizations. Don't be afraid to think outside the box!

No matter what the working arrangement or the issue, trust is central to building effective relationships across and beyond the ecosystem. You may align with some external allies on a limited range of issues and may even disagree on other issues; it is the overall credibility of each contributing individual and their respective organizations that is crucial as groups lend their names to cooperative efforts—particularly those that will be ongoing and highly visible. Centering issues and community impact, rather than the carriers of the message, makes it easier for those with diverse perspectives to be incorporated into unified messaging. This tends to render differences on unrelated matters less important, or even negligible. Professionalism, follow-through, honesty, and good faith are essential characteristics in prospective allies and within your own organizations. Ultimately, the quality of the work and the likelihood of achieving shared goals will be heightened by your growing network. The fact that so much of that work is invisible to the outside world is a nod to the health of your ecosystem, and to the planting you have done, are doing now, and will continue.

NOTES

1. Cathy De Rosa and Jenny Johnson, *From Awareness to Funding: A Study of Library Support in America* (Dublin, OH: OCLC, 2008), www.oclc.org/research/publications/all/funding.html.
2. Unite Against Book Bans, https://UniteAgainstBookBans.org.

CONCLUSION
One Voice, One Future

Eryn Duffee and Michelle Robertson

As we wrap up our exploration of the intricate world of library ecosystems, we reflect on the key insights gained throughout this journey. From understanding the foundational principles of the library ecosystem to delving into the elements of ecosystem thinking, applying those ideas in advocacy, and examining various library types and related organizations, we have uncovered the interconnected web that sustains and empowers our libraries and the people who support them.

Throughout this book, authors from various backgrounds have emphasized the unity that diverse libraries can achieve when bound by common goals and values. The ecosystem continuum consists of four core ideas—leadership, communication, collaboration, and sustainability. These four tenets have emerged as essential components in fostering success in advocacy, intellectual freedom, and broadening our reach and support. We have learned that sustaining advocacy requires long-term commitment and strategic planning.

The chapters dedicated to library types, stakeholders, and potential partners underscore the importance of recognizing each entity's role in the ecosystem. From academic libraries to school libraries and public libraries, we have witnessed the synergy that arises when these different library types work in tandem. We can amplify our benefits and strengthen our standing across our communities by connecting with and building on what each library type offers.

As we explore ecosystems in action, we dispel the myth of going it alone. A journey through the ecosystem showcases the power of collaboration and the collective strength of library warriors standing together. In a world where information is abundant and constantly evolving,

FIGURE C.1 | **The ecosystem web**

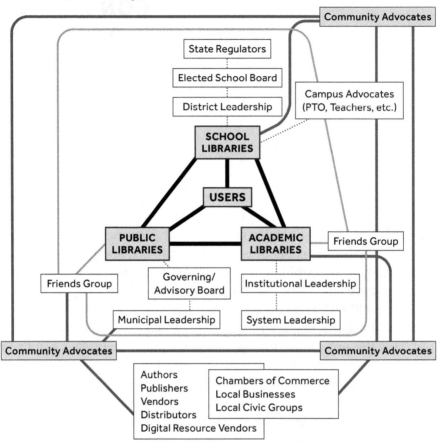

libraries must not only adapt but also support and bolster each other in order to continue our noble work of creating an informed public and strengthening democracy.

The illustrated ecosystem web (figure C.1) highlights the shared points of connection among libraries. Each library connects to others, driven by the tangible benefits of shared resources and the common goal of advocacy. The lines between these libraries form a cohesive network, enveloping users in a readily accessible web of services.

It is crucial to recognize the role that each element in the web plays in advocacy planning. For instance, library boards play a vital role in connecting libraries to the community, and by involving their members in both local and broader advocacy efforts, they build the ecosystem and strengthen advocacy in both public-facing and policy-making arenas.

As another example, most libraries boast Friends groups, whether they are formally organized or are a loose band of volunteers. These Friends groups share commonalities and often collaborate on local initiatives, such as book sales and fundraisers. In some cases, there may be overlapping membership in these groups, such as primary and secondary students transitioning from school libraries to higher education, or active public library supporters who also contribute to the local university or public school.

This book serves as a guide for those navigating the complex landscape of library advocacy. It is a call to action for library leaders and supporters to embrace ecosystem thinking, cultivate collaboration, and champion the values that libraries represent. The future of libraries lies in their ability to adapt, collaborate, and stand united within the dynamic ecosystem they inhabit. Let this be a catalyst for continued growth, innovation, and advocacy in the ever-evolving world of libraries.

The ecosystem surrounds us, an omnipresent force waiting to be harnessed. Your story, distinct yet resonant, unfolds against the backdrop of this intricate environment. Set goals for yourself and others as you start to work together. Internalize the wisdom imparted by the many experienced voices in this book and respond to the call for proactive engagement.

Each day presents an opportunity to shape your unique narrative within the interconnected community. Break from convention, aspire to innovate, and cultivate purposeful connections. As we wrap up this book, we hope the echoes of its wisdom linger, urging you to create your ecosystem and learn how to speak with *One Voice*.

Ecosystem Agenda Building: Information Gathering

Template for Building a Collaborative Advocacy Agenda

Issues that might inform advocacy priorities:

(There are many issues that libraries advocate for. Here are just a few to help you build a list that reflects your organization's priorities.)

Legislative Advocacy	Advocacy for Community Awareness
Funding	Diversity and inclusion
Staffing	Equity of access
Broadband and connectivity	Broadband and connectivity
Digital resources	Digital services
Access	In-person services
Standards	Resources

Ecosystem Agenda Template

Step 1—Gather input from all organizations.

What type of agenda are you building?

___ Legislative ___ Public-Facing Advocacy

---

*These are elements of the ALA Ecosystem Initiative: ONE VOICE: Building a Strong Library Ecosystem (ala.org/advocacy/ala-ecosystem-initiative).

Organization: _____

Priority issues:

1. _____

2. _____

3. _____

Potential overlap between above issues and priorities for other organizations:

- _____

- _____

- _____

Step 2—Consolidate the input.

Take your content above and compare to other organizations.

Ecosystem Agenda Building			
Organization A	Organization B	Oanization C	Organization D
Identify overlapping or related issues from information gathered above.			

Step 3—Develop the shared agenda.

Look at the consolidated input to see how to consolidate these ideas into a prioritized, shared draft agenda.

- _____

- _____

- _____

- _____

Step 4—Send for review and feedback to stakeholders who contributed the foundational information. Refine as needed.

Step 5—Share results, conclusions and plans with stakeholders from all partner organizations.

Ecosystem Agenda Building: Legislative

For the complete template for building a shared agenda, please see Ecosystem Agenda Building: Information Gathering.

Step 1—Gather input from all organizations.

(There are many issues that libraries advocate for. Here are just a few to help you build a list that reflects your organization's priorities.)

Issues that might inform advocacy priorities: Legislative
Funding
Staffing
Broadband and connectivity
Digital resources
Access
Standards

Issue: Funding

Specify the needs of your organization around this issue:

- _____

- _____

- _____

List any overlap you see between your organization and other organizations around this one issue:

- _____

- _____

- _____

Issue: Staffing

Specify the needs of your organization around this issue:

- _____

- _____

- _____

List any overlap you see between your organization and other organizations around this one issue:

- _____

- _____

- _____

Issue: Broadband and connectivity

Specify the needs of your organization around this issue:

- _____

- _____

List any overlap you see between your organization and other organizations around this one issue:

- _____

- _____

- _____

Issue: Digital resources

Specify the needs of your organization around this issue:

- _____

- _____

- _____

List any overlap you see between your organization and other organizations around this one issue:

- _____

- _____

- _____

Issue: Access

Specify the needs of your organization around this issue:

- _____

- _____

- _____

List any overlap you see between your organization and other organizations around this one issue:

- _____

- _____

- _____

Issue: Standards

Specify the needs of your organization around this issue:

- _____

- _____

- _____

List any overlap you see between your organization and other organizations around this one issue:

- _____

- _____

- _____

Issue: [other] _____

Specify the needs of your organization around this issue:

- _____

- _____

- _____

List any overlap you see between your organization and other organizations around this one issue:

- _____

- _____

- _____

Ecosystem Agenda Building:
Advocacy for Community Awareness

For the complete template for building a shared agenda, please see Ecosystem Agenda Building: Information Gathering.

STEP 1—Gather input from all organizations.

(There are many issues that libraries advocate for. Here are just a few to help you build a list that reflects your organization's priorities.)

Issues that might inform advocacy priorities: Advocacy for Community Awareness
Diversity and inclusion
Equity of access
Broadband and connectivity
Digital services
In-person services
Resources

Issue: Diversity and inclusion

Specify the needs of your organization around this issue:

- _____
- _____
- _____

List any overlap you see between your organization and other organizations around this one issue:

- _____
- _____
- _____

Issue: Equity of access

Specify the needs of your organization around this issue:

- _____
- _____
- _____

List any overlap you see between your organization and other organizations around this one issue:

- _____
- _____
- _____

Issue: Broadband and connectivity

Specify the needs of your organization around this issue:

- _____

List any overlap you see between your organization and other organizations around this one issue:

- _____
- _____
- _____

Issue: Digital services

Specify the needs of your organization around this issue:

- _____
- _____
- _____

List any overlap you see between your organization and other organizations around this one issue:

- _____
- _____
- _____

Issue: In-person services

Specify the needs of your organization around this issue:

- _____
- _____
- _____

List any overlap you see between your organization and other organizations around this one issue:

- _____
- _____
- _____

Issue: Resources

Specify the needs of your organization around this issue:

- _____
- _____
- _____

List any overlap you see between your organization and other organizations around this one issue:

- _____
- _____
- _____

Issue: [other] _____

Specify the needs of your organization around this issue:

- _____

- _____

- _____

List any overlap you see between your organization and other organizations around this one issue:

- _____

- _____

- _____

Ecosystem Agenda Building: Consolidate the Input

Take the content from the bullets contributed on Step 1—Gather input from all organizations: Legislative and/or Public-Facing Advocacy.

(Identify repetition and commonalities as indicators of potential collaboration.)

Ecosystem Agenda Building			
Organization A	Organization B	Oanization C	Organization D
Identify overlapping or related issues from information gathered above.			

State and Local Year-Round Advocacy Checklist*

JANUARY ■	FEBRUARY ■	MARCH ■	APRIL ■
• Monthly: share a copy of the library's event calendar and newsletter with elected officials and community leaders. • Sign up for your state association's library legislative event. Have your library story ready to share and follow-up with a thank you to legislators and staff.	• Work with local media to highlight a library program, service, or event that is enabled by state or local funding: www.ala.org/advocacy/media.	• Participate in statewide Library Snapshot Day, or create one for your city/county/school district: www.ala.org/advocacy/snapshotday. • Conduct a mid-session check-in with coalition partners to advance favorable legislation or defeat adverse legislation.	• Celebrate National Library Week, National Library Workers Day, National Bookmobile Day, and/or School Library Month: www.ala.org/conferencesevents/celebrationweeks/natlibraryweek. Ask a state or local governing body to issue a proclamation and tweet your thanks with photos showcasing your library's value to its community.
MAY ■	JUNE ■	JULY ■	AUGUST ■
• Attend a board, county commission, or city council meeting and share something new about the library that positively impacts their constituents. • Invite officials to tour your library or participate in an upcoming event—e.g., summer reading—that aligns with their priorities.	• Join ALA for Annual Conference. If you can't attend in person, follow the conversations on social media channels: @ALAConferences and @ALALibrary. • Attend or schedule advocacy training for the summer.	• Create and distribute a year-in-review infographic (one-page) for elected officials and the public. • Review the legislative session to assess successes, losses, and areas for continued work. • During election years, learn about candidates' positions and educate them about your library.	• Share input across library types for state or regional legislative planning. • Attend in-district events hosted by your state senators & representatives.

*This checklist is an element of the ALA Ecosystem Initiative: ONE VOICE: Building a Strong Library Ecosystem (ala.org/advocacy/ala-ecosystem-initiative).

SEPTEMBER ■	OCTOBER ■	NOVEMBER ■	DECEMBER ■
• Celebrate Library Card Sign-Up Month by engaging community influencers in your public awareness campaign: www.ala.org/conference sevents/celeb rationweeks/card. Partner across library types and with local organizations to highlight the value and impact of libraries.	• Sign up for federal (https://bit.ly/2Enzw9B) & state (https://bit.ly/3ohYl3Y) advocacy alerts. • Confirm your state's legislative session dates and update your advocacy calendar accordingly.	• Ask your trustees to complete the Board Member Survey: https://bit.ly/2UbW95n. • Research newly elected officials to understand their background and priorities. • Review your state organization's legislative agenda & communications plan so that your messaging is aligned with statewide efforts and libraries speak with one voice.	• Welcome new & returning elected officials. Offer your library as a place they can hold meetings/town halls and refer constituents for assistance accessing government services, small business resources, job search support, etc.

Advocacy activities may need to shift in accordance with institutional, organizational, and legislative calendars.

Download at www.ala.org/advocacy/sites/ala.org.advocacy/files/content/stateandlocal/Advocacy%20Checklist.pdf to customize.

#ALAadvocacy

A Comparison of Public, School, and Academic Libraries
Vital to Our Communities*

In neighborhoods, schools, and higher education across the United States, libraries are serving learners of all ages as they pursue both their academic and personal information needs. These institutions, which offer complementary services in the common pursuit of providing top-quality information, access to technology, and safe spaces, often stand aligned in their desire to meet shared goals. These goals include:

- Achieving equity of access to information and resources
- Building a culture of reading
- Supporting lifelong learning
- Creating an engaged, informed citizenry

The library Ecosystem is an integral source of information for all communities. While many libraries pursue the goals listed above in similar ways, it is important to understand the fundamental differences between these institutions that make each a unique and crucial part of the communities they serve. A user of any one of these types of libraries today will become a user of another in the future.

---

*This comparison document is an element of the ALA Ecosystem Initiative: ONE VOICE: Building a Strong Library Ecosystem (ala.org/advocacy/ala-ecosystem-initiative).

Public Library	School Library	Academic Libraries
Mission To provide the tools and free access to support lifelong learning and engagement for all ages and all representations of the wider community.	**Mission** To empower K-12 students to be enthusiastic readers, critical thinkers, skillful researchers, responsible digital global citizens, and ethical users of information.	**Mission** To facilitate all research, scholarship, pedagogy, and learning while upholding tenets of Diversity, Equity, and Inclusion.
Users Any and all members of the public.	**Users** The specific members of a K-12 school community, typically limited to enrolled students and employed faculty and staff.	**Users** Currently enrolled students, faculty, alumni, international scholars, administrators, and local community members.
Staffing Degreed librarians with a Master's level education from an accredited program serve as their library's Information Professionals, alongside non-degreed support staff. Staffing should reflect the diverse communities served by the institution where possible.	**Staffing** Degreed librarians with a Master's level education and specialized education certifications manage effective school library programs with support from non-certified staff. Staffing should reflect the diverse communities served by the institution where possible.	**Staffing** Degreed librarians with specialized certifications and appropriately credentialed staff which reflects the diverse communities served by the institution where possible.
Collections are extensive and typically cover all possible age ranges and reading levels, with a wide selection of topics and material types. Though curated for quality and diversity, the focus of the collection is on providing unhindered access to a wide range of materials for enjoyment and information.	**Collections** are highly curated to include diverse materials almost exclusively published for the designated age range, reading level, and interest of the enrolled students, as well as materials at those levels that also support curricular and classroom activities. Some school library collections may also focus on professional development materials for faculty and staff.	**Collections** facilitate the curation of resources in various formats that support the institution's research goals, including academic and community-oriented activities. Collections will reflect all of our communities, including authors from and experiences of global BIPOC and/or traditionally underrepresented communities. Special Collections may provide exclusive materials and specific focus on rare or uncommon topics.

As the chart above demonstrates, while public, school, and academic libraries are institutions with complementary goals, none could reasonably be expected to stand in the place of the others. Rather, these institutions build upon each other's work by leveraging their unique strengths to address issues of access, equity, and lifelong learning in ways that are neither duplicated nor equaled by any other available resource. **All** libraries remain vital pieces of their respective communities.

The original version of this comparison (https://docs.google.com/document/d/1LJNFYDRefe 4FdH9cA29ECa2VyWMZQQB1vaVWBTOjbvk/edit) was written by the New Jersey Library Association (NJLA) and New Jersey Association of School Librarians (NJASL) which stand united in the conviction that ALL types of libraries are essential. ALA's Committee on Library Advocacy (COLA) Ecosystem Subcommittee has adapted the original document for broader application.

Additional Resources

We include here resources from the American Library Association (ALA), the American Association of School Librarians (AASL), the Association for College & Research Libraries (ACRL), the Public Library Association (PLA), and the Young Adult Library Services Association (YALSA). While every listing here may not have been specifically mentioned in the body of this book, each has the potential to contribute to greater understanding across library types and to strengthening collaborative efforts among local library advocates.

All Libraries

ALA: Addressing Adverse Legislation Toolkit
www.ala.org/advocacy/addressing-adverse-legislation
> This comprehensive guide outlines strategic responses to adverse state-level legislation impacting libraries. Emphasizing proactive engagement, it covers research, strategy, prioritization, collaboration, communication, and adaptability. ALA's involvement includes tracking legislation, providing resources, and offering guidance throughout the advocacy process.

ALA: Advocacy Action Plan Workbook
www.ala.org/advocacy/advocacy-action-planning
> This workbook is intended to help advocates plan effectively towards the realization of specific goals. It is a project of ALA's Committee on Library Advocacy (COLA) and updates the 2009 Advocacy Action Workbook, developed by the American Library Association and United for Libraries.

ALA: State Legislative Toolkit

www.ala.org/advocacy/state-legislative-toolkit

This toolkit offers guidance on preparing for legislative sessions, maintaining advocacy infrastructure, tracking legislation and media, building partnerships and coalitions, engaging with legislators, and addressing adverse legislation.

ALA COLA: Infographic – "Students Reach Greater Heights with School Librarians"

https://ilovelibraries.org/wp-content/uploads/2021/11/students-reach
-greater-heights-with-school-librarians-7.pdf

This valuable infographic shows the tangible benefits of staffing school libraries with certified teacher-librarians. It also provides links to further supportive information.

School Libraries

AASL: Administrators Reflect on School Libraries

www.youtube.com/playlist?list=PL0mICHe7poqbz38I0WAXd7oG4
FFp13AT6

The 2018–2019 AASL president Kathryn Roots Lewis's presidential initiative resulted in the AASL School Leader Collaborative's "Administrators Reflect on School Libraries" videos playlist. These videos are an excellent tool to use in recruiting local school administrators to an ecosystem team.

AASL: Advocacy Definitions

www.ala.org/aasl/advocacy/definitions

These definitions will be useful to every ecosystem participant. For instance, exactly how does advocacy differ from public relations or marketing?

AASL: Advocacy Resources

www.ala.org/aasl/advocacy/resources

These tools include council resolutions, reports, research and statistics, state contacts, position statements, and a bibliography on school and public library partnerships and cooperative programs. It also includes the infographic "Strong School Libraries Build Strong Students."

AASL: Connect with Your Administrators

https://standards.aasl.org/project/transform/

School administrators are one of the largest communities that misunderstand libraries in general and school libraries in general. They are a group of potential library advocates that needs to be included whenever possible.

AASL: Position Statements

www.ala.org/aasl/advocacy/resources/statements

AASL's official position statements include "The Instructional Role of the School Librarian," "The Role of the School Library," and "The School Librarian's Role in Reading," among others.

AASL: Standards Crosswalks

https://standards.aasl.org/project/crosswalks

These crosswalks are an important way to understand the needs of education organizations like the Association for Supervision and Curriculum Development (ASCD) and the International Society for Technology in Education (ISTE) so that they can be counted as library advocates.

School Library Infographics

AASL: "School Librarians Transform Learning"

www.ala.org/sites/default/files/2024-04/AASL_Infographic_FINAL.pdf

Created for the digital supplement "School Libraries Transform Learning," this infographic includes statistics and quotes on school librarians' impact on student learning and leadership within the school. The infographic is freely available for download by members of the media and general public, provided that no alterations are made and the posting is for educational, noncommercial purposes only.

AASL: "Strong School Libraries Build Strong Students"

www.ala.org/sites/default/files/2024-04/AASL_infographic.pdf

> Created by AASL's Legislation Committee, this infographic is freely available for download by members of the media and general public, provided that no alterations are made and the posting is for educational, noncommercial purposes only.

Academic Libraries

ACRL: Academic Library Advocacy Toolkit

https://acrl.libguides.com/advocacytoolkit

> This is a curated collection of resources to equip academic library administrators and library professionals with the resources to advocate for the value, roles, and contributions of academic libraries to their campus communities.

ACRL: Assessment in Action: Demonstrating and Communicating Library Contributions to Student Learning and Success, A Roadshow

www.ala.org/acrl/conferences/roadshows/aiaroadshow

> This is a program for academic librarians who are interested in understanding how to illustrate libraries' impact on student achievement. School librarians might benefit from these ideas as well.

ACRL: Project Outcome for Academic Libraries

https://acrl.projectoutcome.org

> Based on a model developed by the PLA, this free toolkit is designed to help academic libraries understand and share the impact of essential library programs and services by providing simple surveys and an easy-to-use process for measuring and analyzing outcomes.

Public Libraries

ALSC: Public Library & School Library Collaboration Toolkit

www.ala.org/alsc/publications-resources/professional-tools/
school-public-library-partnerships

Both public and school libraries are community centers at heart, with the same goal: to provide a safe, welcoming environment for all patrons and access to information in a variety of formats. When public and school librarians and library workers engage in collaboration, community members reap the benefits. This toolkit includes context and suggestions for creating partnerships of all sizes between them.

PLA: Advocacy Interest Group

This ALA Connect space supports PLA members who are interested in educating their communities about why libraries and librarians are essential in an information society. Please note that participation in PLA interest groups is limited to PLA personal members, and log-in is required.

PLA: Public Libraries Open Possibility

www.ala.org/pla/leadership/advocacy/videos

The PLA and ALA developed a video series showcasing how public libraries open possibilities and transform communities. The videos are intended for the library community, allies, and decision-makers to use as tools to advocate for the future of public libraries. The series is perfect for ecosystem advocates.

Youth Libraries

YALSA: Advocacy Resources

www.ala.org/yalsa/advocacy

Advocacy and activism are strategic goals in YALSA. Ongoing advocacy and updated resources can help ensure that all teens have access to great libraries.

ABOUT THE AUTHORS AND CONTRIBUTORS

Dorcas Hand, MLS, is a retired school librarian from Houston, Texas, who is a co-chair of *Students Need Libraries in Houston ISD*, a grassroots advocacy effort to return school librarians and libraries to all campuses in Houston Independent School District; this local advocacy work has informed much of her ecosystem thinking. She chaired the ALA Ecosystem Initiative Task Force to write the Ecosystem Toolkit and Continuum and remains a member of ALA's COLA Ecosystem Subcommittee, presenting on ecosystem topics often. Dorcas was named a 2024 Texas Library Champion, an award given to those whose influence has changed the landscape of Texas libraries.

Sara Kelly Johns, MLS, a member of ALA's COLA Ecosystem Subcommittee, is an online instructor for Syracuse University's iSchool graduate program. Sara was a longtime school librarian in northern New York's Adirondack Mountains. She was a public library trustee in two libraries and taught an undergraduate library instruction course at the Feinberg Library at the State University of New York, Plattsburgh. A past president of the American Association of School Librarians and the New York Library Association, she is active in ALA Council. With Susan D. Ballard, she coauthored *Elevating the School Library: Building Positive Perceptions through Brand Behavior* (2023).

Michelle Robertson, MLS, PhD, is currently the program coordinator and assistant professor for library media in education at the University of Central Oklahoma. She is a member of ALA's Ecosystem Subcommittee as well as ALA's Public Awareness Committee. She has worked for several years to build the library ecosystem in Oklahoma. Collaboration to build awareness of library services across library communities is her passion.

Eryn Duffee, MLIS, is a teacher librarian near Seattle, Washington, who has led advocacy committees and who founded the Tennessee Library Ecosystem Coalition. Eryn's impactful work earned Tennessee the Gerald Hodges Intellectual Freedom Chapter Award. Recognized with the *Library Journal* Movers & Shakers Award in 2023, Eryn is currently on a mission to give Washington state students equitable access to certified teacher-librarians.

Anthony Chow, PhD, is a full professor and the director of San José State University's School of Information. He was formerly the longtime co-chair of advocacy for the North Carolina Library Association, the state liaison for National Library Legislative Day, the founder of nclibraryadvocacy.org, and a member of ALA's Committee on Library Advocacy.

Megan Murray Cusick, MLIS, has more than two decades of experience championing strategic and creative solutions for stronger and more equitable communities. Prior to launching her own consulting firm, Megan worked in ALA's Public Policy and Advocacy Office, as well as in the Chicago public schools. She has served on a number of nonprofit boards and is a co-founder of the Chicago Teachers Union librarians committee. Megan has presented and published on topics such as advocacy, civic engagement, intellectual freedom, library trends, partnerships, curricular integration, and organizational ecosystems.

Jennifer L. Dean is the director of the Frances Willson Thompson Library and Genesee Historical Collections Center at the University of Michigan-Flint. She holds a PhD in higher, adult, and lifelong education from Michigan State University and an MLIS degree from Wayne State University. Jennifer's research interests include organizational leadership and change management, and she currently serves as a member-at-large on ALA's Learning Round Table Executive Board.

Kathy Lester is a past president of the American Association for School Librarians, a retired school librarian, and an adjunct instructor at Wayne State University. She is also a councilor-at-large for the ALA and has served on several ALA committees, including the Committee on Library

Advocacy, its Ecosystem Subcommittee, and the Committee on Legislation. She is active in her state association, the Michigan Association of School Librarians, where she is a past president and the co-chair of the Advocacy Committee.

Rachel Minkin is currently serving as interim associate dean for teaching and learning at the Michigan State University (MSU) Libraries (in East Lansing). Rachel has also served as the head of reference and discovery services and as an information literacy librarian (both at MSU), a reference and instruction librarian at Lansing Community College, and a reference librarian at the Graduate Theological Union's Flora Lamson Hewlett Library (Berkeley, CA). Rachel earned her MLIS at the University of Pittsburgh. She also holds a Master of Theological Studies degree from Vanderbilt Divinity School (Nashville, TN).

Barbara K. Stripling has held positions as a school librarian, district director of libraries in Arkansas and New York city, and an associate professor in the iSchool at Syracuse University. Barbara has written or edited numerous publications, created the Stripling Model of Inquiry, and developed and published a reimagined Empire State Information Fluency Continuum, a PK-12 continuum of skills that librarians teach to empower students to be lifelong learners. She is a past president of the American Association of School Librarians, the New York Library Association, the American Library Association, and the Freedom to Read Foundation.

Jennifer Alvino Wood is the director of the Windham Public Library in Windham, Maine. She has worked in public libraries for nearly thirty years and is a past attendee of ALA's Leadership Symposium. Jennifer is a past president of the New England Library Association and the Maine Library Association and has held various other library association positions, including chair of ALA's Chapter Relations Committee. She is currently the Maine ALA councilor and the co-chair of COLA's Ecosystem Subcommittee. She lives in Sebago, Maine, with her husband, two boys, and two fluffy dogs.

INDEX

A

academic libraries, 4, 22*t*, 23-24, 70, 135-143

Academic Library Advocacy Toolkit (ACRL), 9

access, 16-17, 18-20, 23, 25, 53, 148-149, 151-152, 165, 166

ACLU of Maine, 168

ACRL Speaks Out, 9

Act to Establish a Rating System for Books in School Libraries, An, 168-169

Act to Prohibit the Dissemination of Obscene Materials by Public Schools, An, 168

action plans, 101, 159

advisory boards, 164

advocacy
 academic libraries and, 137-138
 basics of, 88-89
 best practices for, 94-97
 calendar for, 81, 204
 collaboration and, 185-186
 communication and, 58-59
 defining, 8-10, 88-89
 Five P's of, 159-160, 160*fig*
 for funding, 192
 leading from life and, 87-98
 legislative, 66-67, 99-110, 155, 156-158, 166-168, 219-220
 position statements and, 62-63
 principles of, 92-93
 for public awareness, 67
 public-facing, 12-13
 school libraries and, 152-153, 155-159
 strategic, 123-124, 128-129
 themes for, 90

"Advocacy Action Plan Workbook," 8, 215

Advocacy Bootcamps, 93

Advocacy Strategy Framework, 90, 90*fig*

advocates and supporters, ix*fig*, 182

affiliate organizations, 173-177

Agenda Building Templates. *See* Ecosystem Agenda Building Templates

agendas
 developing, 66-67
 implementing, 219-220
 legislative, 99-100, 169

American Association of School Librarians (AASL), vii-viii, 9, 146-147, 149

American Indian Library Association (AILA), 175, 176

American Library Association, 113, 114, 123, 124, 129, 218

American Rescue Plan Act, 152

Anchor Standard II, 121

Arkansas Library Leadership Institute (ALL-In) program, 196

Asian/Pacific American Librarians Association (APALA), 175, 176-177

asks, 95

Association of College and Research Libraries (ACRL), 9, 138-139

Association of Library and Information School Education (ALISE), 174-175

Association of Rural and Small Libraries, 175

audience, 91

Austin (TX) Public Library, 112

B

Banned Books Week Coalition, 113
Beginning level, 30
being present, 160, 160*fig*
Beloved (Morrison), 71
Bill of Rights, 25
Bingham, Elizabeth, 92–93
BIPOC communities, 175
Black Caucus of the American Library
   Association (BCALA), 174, 175
Blue Willow Book Shop, 187
boards of trustees, 164
book challenges, 71–73, 116, 120, 125–126
"brave" spaces, 121
broadband adoption, 129
businesses, education ecosystem and, 154
Butler, Amalia E., 175

C

calendars, 81, 204
Cedar Rapids (IA) Library's Trustee Advo-
   cacy Committee, 186
censorship, 71–73, 81, 120, 123, 125–126,
   129, 184, 186, 193–194
Center for an Informed Public, 121
Center for Media Literacy, 121
challenged materials policy, 125–126
change agents, 51–52, 78
Chicago Public Schools, 125–126
Chief Officers of State Library Agencies
   (COSLA), 177
Chinese American Library Association
   (CALA), 176
Chrislip, David, 68
"Citizens-Save-Libraries Power Guide," 184
climate resiliency, 18
coalitions, 216–218, 219*fig*
collaboration
   academic libraries and, 137
   advocacy and, 185–186
   common goals and, 15
   definition of, 216
   examples of, 70–73, 201–209
   intellectual freedom and, 122–123
   leadership and, 52
   as pillar, 10–11, 29, 31*fig*, 38–40*fig*,
      38–41

rubric for, 69–70
silos and, 12
state level, 192–196
success and, 65–75
collection development, 112, 118, 119–120,
   124–125, 128, 166
collection-mapping, 119
college libraries, 23–24
Comic Book Legal Defense Fund, 113, 123
committee hearings, 107–108
Committee on Criminal Justice and Public
   Safety (Maine), 168
Committee on Education and Cultural
   Affairs, 168
Committee on Library Advocacy (COLA),
   vii, 8, 101, 119
Common Sense Education, 121
communication
   with advocacy allies, 58–59
   avenues for, 56–57
   bidirectional, 56
   coalitions and, 217
   external, 37
   intellectual freedom and, 122–123
   internal, 37
   leadership and, 50, 52–53
   legislative-facing, 60–62
   online, 56–57
   as pillar, 10–11, 29, 31*fig*, 32, 34–36*fig*
   position statements and, 62–63
   public-facing, 59–60
   relationship-building and, 153
   strong, 55–63
   sustainability and, 80
community, 3, 6, 20, 165
Community Anchor Program, 115
community college libraries, 23–24
community groups, 154
Community Tool Box, 68
community-building, 116
Comparison of Public, School, and Academic Libraries, xii, 37, 81, 140, 149, 152,
   237–239
conferences, 57
confidentiality, 20, 24, 59, 127. *See also*
   privacy
constituents, advocacy and, 95–96
consultants, library, 178

contact information, 95
contacts, organization of, 37
continuity, 103
Core Values of Librarianship, 15, 16, 153, 165
corporate entities, 183
Council of State School Library Consultants (CSSLC), 177-178
Cusick, Megan, 89

D

data, advocacy and, 91-92, 96, 105-106, 105*fig*, 139-141, 156
database subscriptions, shared, 192
decision-makers, definition of, 31
decision-making
    advocacy best practices and, 97
    collaboration and, 68
    psychology of, 93-94
Delaware Literacy Alliance, 196
democracy
    access and, 25
    information literacy and, 19
    intellectual freedom and, 115-116
determination, 50
Dietrich, Cindy, 94
digital citizenship, 121
digital inclusion, 129
digital public library ecosystem, 170-171, 170*fig*
"Digital Public Library Ecosystem 2023" report, 170
dissension, 46, 82-83
District of Columbia (DC) public schools, 114
diverse approaches, 97
diversity, 19, 20, 113-114, 119, 124-125, 181-189, 220
Douglas County (Colorado) Libraries, 93

E

e-books, 171
ecosystem
    definition of, xi, 3
    diagram of, 222*fig*
    dynamics of, 80-81
Ecosystem Agenda Building Templates, xii, 41, 67, 981, 100, 106, 225-234

Ecosystem Continuum
    adapting, 47
    advocacy best practices and, 153
    continual work on, 46-47
    organizational models and, 45-46
    overview of, 29-32
    pillars of, 10-12, 29, 31*fig*, 32-45
    resources related to, 81
    role of, 7
Ecosystem Initiative, 3
Ecosystem Initiative Task Force, vii
ecosystem team, definition of, 30
Ecosystem Toolkit, vii-ix, 7, 8, 68, 81
education, 20
education associations, 154
education ecosystem, 153-154
educational anchors, 6
empathy, 50
Empire State Information Fluency Continuum, 121
equitable access policies, 127-128
equity, 16-17, 18, 53, 113, 124, 149, 151-152, 165
"E's of Libraries, The" (program), 184
evaluation, 46
Every Student Succeeds Act (ESSA), vii-viii, 152
Evolving level, 30
executive sessions, 108
external ecosystems, 119, 120
external partners, 135, 138

F

First Amendment, 25, 59, 112, 119, 124, 185, 186
"First Years Meet the Frames," 138
flexibility, 50
Foote, Carolyn, 123
foundations, 182-183
FReadom Fighters, 123, 186
Freedom to Read Foundation, 113, 129
Friends groups, 182-183, 185-186, 196, 223
Friends of Libraries, New York Library Association (NYLA), 186
Friends of South Carolina Libraries (FOSCL), 185

Friends of Tennessee Libraries (FOTL), 185, 208
Friends of the Saint Paul Public Library, 186
From Funding to Awareness, 214
funding
    advocacy for, 192
    attacks on, 166-167

G

genealogy collections, 24
goals
    common, 19-26, 20*fig*, 53, 217
    legislative advocacy and, 101
Godwin, Jo, 120
going it alone, myth of, 211-220, 221
Gorman, Amanda, 74
governance structures, for public libraries, 164-165
governing boards, 164
gratitude/thank yous, 62, 159

H

Hartley, C. A., 93
Highly Effective level, 30
historical record, 20

I

implementation, 109-110
inclusion, 113, 124
Indiana Library Federation, 195
Indiana State Library, 195
inequities
    addressing, 115
    in school libraries, 152
infographics, 105-106, 105*fig*, 109, 149
information literacy, 19, 21, 53, 71, 104, 115, 149-151, 207
information specialists, school librarians as, 149
Infrastructure Investment and Jobs Act, 129
Inouye, Alan, 89, 97
inquiry skills, 20, 21
Inslee, Jay, 104
Institute of Museum and Library Services (IMLS), 115, 155

instruction, 120-121
instructional partners, school librarians as, 148-149
integrity, 50
intellectual freedom
    advocacy allies and, 58
    attacks on, 167-168
    challenges to, 81, 140
    collaboration and, 71-73
    community college libraries and, 24
    as core value, 16-20, 25, 165
    demands of, 117-118
    ecosystem framework and, 111-132
    information specialists and, 149
    public libraries and, 23
    public-facing communication and, 59-60
    tools to support, 184-185
interlibrary loan, 193
internal ecosystems, 118-119
International Literacy Association, 148
International Society for Technology in Education (ISTE), 121
Internet2, 115
interpersonal advocacy skills, 90, 96

J

Jacobs, Melissa, 122
Jefferson, Julius C., Jr., 175
Joint Council of Librarians of Color (JCLC), 176

K

Kachel, Deborah E., 151-152
Kentucky State Library, 196
Kirchner, Terry, 92-93
Knox, Emily, 117-118
Koehler, Valerie, 187

L

Lafayette College, 113
Lance, Keith Curry, 151-152
Larson, Carl, 68
LaRue, Jamie, 93, 94-95
law libraries, 24

leadership
  building and sustaining, 49-54
  changing, 50-51
  characteristics for, 50
  collaborative, 68
  ecosystem perspective on, 51
  levels of, 51-52
  as pillar, 10, 29, 31*fig*, 32
  rubric for, 33*fig*
  school librarians and, 148
  shared, 67-68
  state level, 191-197
  sustainability and, 77
  sustaining, 79-80
  warrior, 130
learning
  culture of, 21
  lifelong, 20, 164
  love of, 20, 21
leave-behinds, 95
legislative advocacy, 66-67, 81, 99-110,
  155-158, 166-168, 219-220
legislative agendas, 99-100
legislative efforts, collaboration and,
  70-71
legislative-facing communication, 60-62
"Leverage Libraries to Achieve Digital
  Equity for All," 129
Library Bill of Rights, 165
library consultants, 178
library ecosystem
  definition of, 145-146
  overview of, 3-13
  values and goals and, 15-26
Library Friends, Trustees, and Advocates
  Round Table (LiFTA), 183
Library Journal, 72
Library Legislative Day, 169
library practice, 118-119
"Library Privacy Guidelines for Learning
  Management Systems," 127
Library Services and Technology Act
  (LSTA), 5
lifelong learning, 20, 164
lip service, 107
literacy, 145, 148
local core values, 18-19

M
Maine Association of School Libraries
  (MASL), 168
Maine Council for English Language Arts,
  168
Maine Humanities Council, 168
Maine Library Association (MLA), 168, 169
Maine Library Trustee Handbook, 166
Maine Taxpayer Bill of Rights, 167
Maine Writers & Publishers, 168
marketing, 7, 91
Massachusetts Board of Library Commis-
  sioners, 191, 193-194, 195
materials selection policy, 124-125. *See also*
  collection development
media literacy, 114-115, 121
Media Literacy and Anchor Standard III,
  121
medical libraries, 24
membership, sustaining, 80
messaging, clear, 106
Minnesota Association of Library Friends,
  186
Moms for Liberty, 208
Monroe (GA) Area High School, 125
Morrison, Toni, 71
Murphy, Laura, 71
mycorrhizal networks, 212

N
Naperville (IL) Public Library, 124-125
narrative, advocacy and, 91-92, 96, 156
National Association for Media Literacy
  Education (NAMLE), 121, 176
National Association of Social Workers
  Maine Chapter, 168
National Associations of Librarians of Color
  (NALCo), 175-176
National Coalition Against Censorship, 113
National Storytelling Network (NSN), 178
Neal, Jim, viii
Nebraska Library Association, 195-196
Nebraska School Library Association
  (NSLA), 195-196
neutrality, 117-118
Nevada State Library and Archives, 195

New Hampshire Library Trustee Association, 185

New Jersey Association of School Librarians (NJASL), 70-71, 138, 206-207

New Jersey Library Association (NJLA), 70, 207

New York Library Association (NYLA), 12, 186

News Literacy Project, 121

non-librarians, building coalition including, 181-182

North Carolina Library Association (NCLA), 88

North Dakota State Library, 194

NYCSLIST, 122-123

O

Obama, Barack, vii

Office for Intellectual Freedom, 120

Oklahoma Department of Libraries (ODL), 195

Oklahoma Library Association (OLA), 204-205

Oklahoma State School Boards Association (OSSBA), 204-205

omnidirectionality, 104

One Voice

framework of, 5, 5*fig*

pillars and, 10

organizational models, 45-46

P

Palesky, Carol, 167

parent groups, 154, 183

Parental Rights in Education bill (Florida), 129

participating organization, definition of, 30

partnerships, 216

Patmos Library, Michigan, 25-26

patrons, key services and, 21-24, 22*t*

Peet, Lisa, 91

Penguin Random House, 187

PEN/PEN America, 113, 123

persistence, 160, 160*fig*

personas, 7-8

Pionke, JJ, 90

Pitkin County Library (Aspen, CO), 115

policies, 123-128

policymakers, definition of, 31

politeness, 160, 160*fig*

Poole's Principle of Least Effort, 94

population, 3

position statements, 62-63

positivity, 160, 160*fig*

preparation, 160, 160*fig*

preservation, 20

privacy, 16-17, 18, 20, 24, 127

problem-solving, collaborative, 68

professional development, 194

professionalism, 18

program administrators, 149

programs and services, intellectual freedom and, 121-122

Project Outcome for Academic Libraries, 139

Property Tax Cap, 167

public access, 20

public awareness, 67, 158, 184

public good, as value, 16, 18, 20, 165

public libraries, 4, 22*t*, 23, 114-115, 163-172

Public Library Association (PLA), 9, 88, 139, 174

Public Policy and Advocacy Office, 218

public relations, 7, 107. *See also* communication

public-facing communication, 59-60

R

Raab, H. A., 93

REFORMA: The National Association to Promote Library and Information Services to Latinos and the Spanish-Speaking, 176

regulations, 123-124, 128-129

relationship-building, 90, 95, 96, 103-104, 153, 213

representatives/representation, defining, 45

resilience, 50

resonance, 95

resources, advocating for, 91

Rettig, Jim, viii, 5

return on investment (ROI), 91

right to read, 25, 53, 71-73, 112, 113, 118, 148
Round Rock Black Parents Association, 186

S

safe havens, 6, 116, 121, 151
Santos, Sharon Tomika, 103-104
school administrator groups, 154
school libraries, 4, 21-23, 22*t*, 70, 114-115,
    120-121, 125, 129, 145-162, 183-184
Seasholes, Craig, 103-104, 106
Seattle (WA) Public Library, 113
service and professionalism, 18
"Share Your Story," 185
sharing economy, 164
site visits, 103-104
Social and Civic Responsibility, 121
social media, 56, 56*fig*, 93, 127
social responsibility, 17, 20
Something, Someday (Gorman), 74
special libraries, 4-5, 24
sponsorship, 106-107
stakeholders
    aligning message to, 158-159
    educating, 159
    knowing, 157-158
    strength with, 65-66
State and Local Year-Round Advocacy
    Checklist, 81, 235-236
State Legislative Toolkit, 215
state level leadership, 191-197
state library agencies (SLA), 191-197
State Local Year-Round Advocacy Check-
    list, xii
story, power of, 94-95, 96
strategic advocacy, 123-124, 128-129
strengths, assessing, 69
Stripling, Barbara, 173-174
student success/achievement, 138-139, 156
"Students Reach Greater Heights with
    School Libraries," 149-151, 150*fig*
success, measuring, 82
succession planning, 45, 79
summer programs, 194
"super supporters," 214
surveying member groups, 100
sustainability
    building, 78-83

closer look at, 25-26
continuum of, 41, 45
as core value, 16, 18, 20, 165
facilitating, 77-78
importance of, 77-78
as pillar, 11, 29, 31*fig*
process of, 77-83
rubric for, 42-44*fig*

T

TABOR, 167
tagline, power of, 94-95
Talk Story program, 176-177
TALL Texans Leadership Development
    Institute, 196
teachers, librarians as, 147-148
team building, 97
Telling Room, The, 168
Tennessee Association of School Librarians
    (TASL), 185, 208
Tennessee Library Association (TNLA),
    185, 208
Tennessee Library Ecosystem Consortium
    (TLEC), 185, 208-209
"Terms and Definitions Related to Intellec-
    tual Freedom & Censorship," 185
testifying at hearings, 108
Texas A&M University, 140
Texas Freedom to Read Project, 186
Texas Library Association, 18-19, 109, 183,
    196
third spaces, 116
time management, 46
Toward Gigabit Libraries Toolkit, 115
trust, 220
trustees, 164, 182, 186
Turning the Page advocacy training mate-
    rials, 9

U

union catalogs, 193
Unite Against Book Bans (UABB), 6, 71-73,
    114, 182, 186, 187-188, 218
United for Libraries, 182-185, 187-188
universal design, 128
university libraries, 23-24

University of Kansas, 67–68
University of Washington's Center for an
  Informed Public, 121, 205–206
User Experience Group, University of
  Washington, 7
user experience (UX), 7
Utah Academic Library Consortium
  (UALC), 202–203
Utah Cultural Alliance, 203
Utah Educational Library Media Associa-
  tion (UELMA), 201–203
Utah Libraries: Keystone of Healthy Democ-
  racy, Student Success, and Prosperous
  Communities, 202–203
Utah Library Association (ULA), 201–203
Utah Parents United, 202

V

Vaaler, Alyson, 140
value, showcasing, 90–91, 96
Value of Academic Libraries, The
  (VAL report), 139
values
  common/shared, 7, 122
  core, 15–19, 16*fig*, 165–166, 219*fig*
Varga, Lisa, 71–72, 73*fig*, 213
vendors, 187
Virginia Association of School Librarians
  (VAASL), 71–73
Virginia Library Association (VLA), 71–73,
  213
virtual events, 57
vision, 50
vocabulary, aligning, 39, 68, 153

W

Ward, Jennifer, 7–8
warrior leadership, 130
Washington Library Association (WLA),
  102, 104, 109, 205–206
Washington Library Media Association
  (WLMA), 205–206
Washington State Legislature, 101–102,
  104, 108–109
webinars, 57, 109
Wyoming State Library, 193

Y

Young Adult Library Services Association
  (YALSA), 9
Youngkin, Glenn, 72
youth services, 194